Big Girls Do Cry

Big Girls Do Cry

PREVENTING CHURCH HURT

AMY LEIGH MOORE

Big Girls Do Cry by Amy Leigh Moore
Copyright © 2018 by Amy Leigh Moore
All Rights Reserved.
ISBN: 978-1-59755-467-1

Published by: ADVANTAGE BOOKS™
Longwood, Florida, USA
www.advbookstore.com

This book and parts thereof may not be reproduced in any form, stored in a retrieval system or transmitted in any form by any means (electronic, mechanical, photocopy, recording or otherwise) without prior written permission of the author, except as provided by United States of America copyright law.

Unless otherwise noted, Scripture quotations are from the New King James Version, copyright © 1982. Used by permission of Thomas Nelson, Inc. All rights reserved.

Library of Congress Catalog Number: 2018938230
1. Religion / Christian Life / Inspirational
2. Religion / Christian Life / Personal Growth

First Printing: March 2018
18 19 20 21 22 23   10 9 8 7 6 5 4 3 2 1
Printed in the United States of America

Table of Contents

Introduction: Preserving our World 5
    Chapter 1: The Anointing and Power in the Church 7
    Chapter 2: Church Based on Relationships 11
    Chapter 3: Church Hurt 19
    Chapter 4: The Cornerstone of the Church 27
    Chapter 5: The Full Foundation of the Church 31
    Chapter 6: The Pastor 37
    Chapter 7: The Needs of the People 45
    Chapter 8: Practical Application 57
    Chapter 9: The Benevolence Ministry 71
    Chapter 10: Evaluation 77
    Chapter 11: Warnings and Rewards for Shepherds 81
    Chapter 12: Expected Results 85
    Chapter 13: To Those Who Have Been Hurt in the Church 87
Conclusion: Stop the Insanity 99
Loving By Faith Bible Study 101
End Notes 225

Amy Leigh Moore

Introduction

Preserving our World

Many Christians I know, including myself, are concerned about where our society is heading. It seems to many that our country is rotting from within. Homosexuality is legal and blatant and anyone that says that homosexuality is a sin is threatened with jail time or a major fine levied on their business. Planned Parenthood is allegedly selling baby parts from aborted babies. Almost every major city in the US has seen rioting in the last few years or so and it seems that discontent is the major theme on Facebook.

How do we stop the spoiling of a great society? Well, Jesus showed us how to prevent this rotting of society.

Matthew 5:13 "You are the salt of the earth; but if the salt loses its flavor, how shall it be seasoned? It is then good for nothing but to be thrown out and trampled underfoot by men."

Salt is a preservative so what Jesus is saying is that we (Christians) are to be the preservative of our society. America is known as a Christian nation. If that is so then why is our society rotting from within? Could it be that the salt has lost its saltiness and can no longer be the preservative it is supposed to be? If the Church has lost its saltiness, then the Church is in danger of being thrown out and trampled underfoot. In fact, God says that His Church will be the first to be judged.

1 Peter 4:17 "For the time has come for judgment to begin at the house of God; and if it begins with us first, what will be the end of those who do not obey the gospel of God?"

The Church that has lost its saltiness will be judged by being thrown out and trampled underfoot. God is coming back for a pure and undefiled bride and that bride is a salty Church that is preserving the world around it.

My late husband loved Country ham, which is salt preserved ham. This ham did not have to be refrigerated because the salt preserved it at room temperature. If the salt that preserved that ham somehow became just like the ham, then could it preserve that ham? No, it couldn't. Salt preserves the ham precisely because it is different than the ham.

I believe that the Church has lost its saltiness and that is the reason that our society is rotting from within. This is not the fault of our Government. God does not say that the Government is to be the salt of the earth. Jesus says that we, the Church, are to be the salt of the earth. This means we must be different then the world around us.

In fact, I am not the only person to have written about this. Bill Hull, in his book, "The Complete Book of Discipleship" talks about doing Church the Jesus way or the consumer way and he says that most of our Churches are doing Church the consumer way instead of the Jesus way. Doing Church in the consumer way has caused us to become just like the world around us and thus we have lost our saltiness. If we do not change how we do Church, God will throw us out and we will be trampled underfoot.

So how do we start doing Church in the Jesus way? I believe this has start with the foundation of the Church. If we ask most people what the foundation of the Church is they would, more than likely, say Jesus is the foundation of the Church. And even though that is true it is an incomplete answer. Jesus is the Cornerstone, not the full foundation of the Church. This book will examine what I believe the full foundation of the Church should be and how to rebuild those foundations. When we build the Church on a complete foundation, we can then preserve our world again.

As I was healing from my own Church hurt, I started researching other people's Church hurt and I started asking God, "Why is this happening?" and "How do we stop it from happening?" God started to show me bits and pieces of the puzzle and after six years of asking and searching, this book has brought the pieces together and formed the answer that I was looking for. Is it the only answer out there? No. But it is the answer that I needed. This is a very different approach to Church hurt then what I have read from other authors. Most of the other approaches to Church hurt I have read are about healing Church hurt AFTER it happens. I want to prevent it from happening in the first place. I believe if we start to put this answer into practice, we could prevent a lot more people from being hurt in the Church and bring the saltiness back into our Churches.

Chapter 1

The Anointing and Power in the Church

Acts 5:12-16 "And through the hands of the apostles many signs and wonders were done among the people. And they were all with one accord in Solomon's Porch. Yet none of the rest dared join them, but the people esteemed them highly. And believers were increasingly added to the Lord, multitudes of both men and women, so that they brought the sick out into the streets and laid them on beds and couches, that at least the shadow of Peter passing by might fall on some of them. Also, a multitude gathered from the surrounding cities to Jerusalem, bringing sick people and those who were tormented by unclean spirits, and they were all healed."

Most Pastors that I know would love to have this type of Power in their Churches. But even though they may crave this type of Power many of them don't believe that this type of Power is available to the Church today. I have heard Pastors preach that the Power that we see in the Church in Acts was a special Anointing to kick start the Church and that it has now passed away. Well, I agree with that to a certain extent. Yes, I do believe that Anointing was a special Anointing to kick start the Church but I disagree that it has passed away. There is nowhere in Scripture that says this Power and Anointing was only for the Church in Acts. I believe our world needs this kind of Anointing and Power even more now than it did back in the times of the disciples. It is only through this type of Power and Anointing that we can truly be the salt of the earth and preserve our rotting society.

Deuteronomy 10:17"For the LORD your God is God of gods and Lord of lords, the great God, mighty and awesome, who shows no partiality nor takes a bribe."

***Job 34:19** "Yet He is not partial to princes, nor does He regard the rich more than the poor; For they are all the work of His hands.*

***Acts 10:34-35** "Then Peter opened his mouth and said: "In truth I perceive that God shows no partiality. But in every nation whoever fears Him and works righteousness is accepted by Him."*

***Romans 2:11** "For there is no partiality with God."*

God does not play favorites as can be seen in these verses. If God was willing to pour out this type of Power and Anointing on the Disciples but not willing to give it to us, then doesn't that show partiality? I think we have seen this Power periodically through some amazing men and women of God but since the times of the disciples, we have not seen it on a regular basis nor as strongly as we saw it with the disciples. Why is that? I believe this has happened because we have not done what the disciples did. God has certain prerequisites that must be met before He pours out that kind of Power and Anointing on a regular basis. If we would do what they did, then we would see a similar Anointing and Power in our Churches. Will that Anointing and Power look the same as it did for the Apostles? I doubt it because we live in a different time and in a different culture. But it will be similar.

So, the next question is: what did the disciples do that we are not doing?

***Acts 2:43-47** "Then fear came upon every soul, and many wonders and signs were done through the apostles. Now all who believed were together, and had all things in common, and sold their possessions and goods, and divided them among all, as anyone had need. So, continuing daily with one accord in the temple, and breaking bread from house to house, they ate their food with gladness and simplicity of heart, praising God and having favor with all the people. And the Lord added to the church daily those who were being saved."*

***Acts 4:34-35** "Nor was there anyone among them who lacked; for all who were possessors of lands or houses sold them, and brought the proceeds of the things that were sold, and laid them at the apostles' feet; and they distributed to each as anyone had need."*

The Disciples were not forcing the wealthy to sell their land and give the money to them so everyone had enough. This was not communism nor was it socialism. Those two systems are government systems that force people to give up what they have so someone who has less can have more. These systems do not work, as has been proven repeatedly in the world's history.

What we see in the book of Acts was God's love in action. God is love so the Anointing He pours out will be based in love. God poured His love for the poor out on the wealthy in these verses. The wealthy loved the poor so much that they willingly gave up their property to make sure that "no one lacked" anything. Can we say the same thing about our Churches in the US today?

But the wealthy selling their property to help the needy was not "what" this Church did. It was "how" they did it. This distinction is very important because once we understand "what" they did, then we can do the same thing but in a different way. What the disciples did was to understand and accept their responsibility of being true shepherds for the people. Being a true shepherd means that the leadership cares for ALL the needs of the people until "no one lacks anything", just as they did in the book of Acts. We haven't seen this type of anointing because many of our Church leaders have rejected this responsibility because they think it is too much for them. God will not do His part unless and until we do our part. So, if we want to see that type of anointing, we must do what they did.

So how do we accomplish the same thing in today's world? Meeting ALL the needs of everyone until "no one lacked anything" seems overwhelming and impossible. I believe that it can be done but to do this means we must re-evaluate the foundations of the Church. This must start with the leadership but the people must be involved in the process as well. I fully believe that if we as a Church would start to try, in faith, to accomplish the same thing the Church in Acts did, then God will show up and His Anointing and Power will fall and will fill in the places where we fail.

Amy Leigh Moore

Chapter 2

Church Based on Relationships

The first step in re-evaluating the Church foundations is to ask whether your Church is based on relationships or based on rituals. Every time I mention to someone that I am not in a Church, the very first thing they say to me is that I should not "forsake the assembling of ourselves together". That comes from Hebrews 10:25 so I would like to examine those verses more closely.

Hebrews 10:24-25 "And let us consider one another in order to stir up love and good works, 25 not forsaking the assembling of ourselves together, as is the manner of some, but exhorting one another, and so much the more as you see the Day approaching."

Notice the wording in these verses. We are to *consider* one another and *exhort* one another. This is about relationship, NOT about ritual. How can we consider one another and exhort one another if we are all sitting in rows, watching a show on stage and there is no interaction between anyone? God wants the Church based on relationship not on ritual. Relationship means that we rejoice with people in the good times and support them in the bad times. I don't see many Churches doing that, I see a lot of rituals. Every Church has rituals and rituals are not necessarily a bad thing unless those rituals come before the relationships.

Imagine throwing a birthday party for your child. That birthday party is a ritual that celebrates your child and the relationship you have with your child. Now imagine crashing a birthday party for a child that you do not know. The free cake and ice cream may taste good but the party has no real meaning to you because you do not have a relationship with the person that is being celebrated.

Our Sunday morning services should be the same thing as the birthday party you throw for your own child. It should be a celebration of our relationship with God and with the other people of God. But in many of our Churches, Sunday morning service is like attending a Birthday party of a person you don't know. The music is good and the light shows are fun but it has no meaning because it is a ritual with no relationship. Especially in our mega-Churches, we sit in rows next to people we do not know and watch a show being performed on stage.

This was not why Jesus died an excruciating death. Jesus died to bring us into relationship with God and to allow us to have closer relationships with one another through Him. That reason can be seen in the tearing of the curtain in the Temple when Jesus died.

Matthew 27:51 "Then, behold, the veil of the temple was torn in two from top to bottom; and the earth quaked, and the rocks were split"

When the curtain was torn, it symbolized the tearing of the barriers that kept us from having that close relationship with God and with other believers. When we reduce that relationship into a Sunday morning ritual, we demean what Jesus did on our behalf.

I had a friend say that the main reason for going to church is to worship God. I understand her thinking but I disagree with it. God does not reside only in the church building; He is everywhere so we can worship Him anywhere we are. When Jesus was asked where worship was to take place: The Temple or the mountain, he said that people would worship in Spirit and in Truth. The place is not important so that cannot be the main reason for going to church. I believe the main reason for going to church is the relationships with other people. Jesus commanded us to love one another and to "bear one another's burdens". That should be the main reason for going to church; not to worship God. Living this life alone is not impossible but it is very hard. I know because I have done it for many years. It was not my choice to live the Christian Life by myself but it happened because no one was willing to "bear my burdens" with me so I was alone. If church is not the place where we can come together to love and help one another then what is the point of the church at all?

The American Church has taken as much relationship out of the Church as they can. People sit in rows and watch a show being played out on stage by the choir and the Pastor. There is really no interaction in our Church services on Sunday mornings. Most Churches even stream their services online so they can be accessible 24 hours a day. Since we can watch the show online, why should we go to Church at all anymore? Church should never be about watching a show on stage; it should be about relationships with other believers. But most Churches are no longer based on

Chapter 2: Church Based on Relationships

relationship because there is no interaction. Without any interaction, then how can any relationship develop?

So how do we bring interaction back into the Sunday morning service? To answer that question, I will borrow an idea from the entertainment industry. I am a huge Star Trek fan and even though I have never been to a convention I have watched them on YouTube. One of the favorite events at a Star Trek convention is the discussion panel. The stars of a show, such as Star Trek, The Next Generation, will be sitting on stage and will answer questions from the fans in the audience. This is one of the best ways for the fans to connect to the stars. Many of Jesus' teachings were a result of people asking Him questions so this approach is not only successful in the entertainment industry but Jesus also used it successfully.

Why can't we do the same thing in the Church during the Sunday morning service? Instead of the senior Pastor preaching his normal sermon, a discussion panel could be set up on stage with all the Pastors of the Church on the panel. This could happen for one Sunday every two to three months. In large Churches, the panel could include the Youth Pastor, the Senior Pastor, the Children's Pastor, and the Benevolence Pastor. Then the ushers would be standing out in the congregation holding microphones. The people would raise their hands if they had a question and they can only ask that question when they are handed the microphone. After they asked their question then one of the Pastors would answer that question using the Bible.

This would require that the Pastors know their Scripture and be willing to think quickly to be able to answer these questions. The questions would be recorded for later viewing and the Senior Pastor could use the questions that are asked as a guide for his subsequent sermons. This is one way for the Pastor to connect with his congregation and know what their needs may be. And then in subsequent sermons he could more fully answer those questions. This way the Pastor starts to meet the Spiritual needs of his people. How can a Pastor know what the people need if he never communicates with them?

One of the protests of this idea may be that it would cause chaos in the Church and God is not a God of chaos but of order. Yes, God is a God of order but why does something new have to automatically be assumed that it will bring chaos to the Church? The entertainment industry uses this strategy without any chaos so why do we think it would bring chaos into the Church? If something like this would be introduced in our Sunday morning services, it would keep people involved and a lot less people would fall asleep during the service. This would bring some interaction into our Sunday morning services.

Relationships not only need interaction but they need both sides to work together and for each person to do their part. Relationships have two sides to them and both sides must do their parts for those relationships to be successful. There are multiple examples of this in Scripture.

Ephesians 5:22 "Wives, submit to your own husbands, as to the Lord."

Ephesians 5:25 "Husbands, love your wives, just as Christ also loved the church and gave Himself for her"

Ephesians 6:1-4 "Children, obey your parents in the Lord, for this is right. 2 "Honor your father and mother," which is the first commandment with promise: "that it may be well with you and you may live long on the earth. And you, fathers, do not provoke your children to wrath, but bring them up in the training and admonition of the Lord."

Notice that these verses give both sides of the marriage, and parent/child relationship. Both sides must do their part for these relationships to be successful. So, who does their part first? I have heard some Pastors say that because the job of the follower comes first in those verses that the follower must do their part first. I disagree.

Do you remember the childhood game "follow the leader"? This game is a perfect illustration of who is to do their job first; the leader or the follower. In this game, the children are in a line and the person at the head of the line is the leader. The leader leads the rest of the kids in a line and the children that follow the leader must copy what the leader does. So, if the leader skips then the rest of the kids skip. If the leader runs then the rest of the children run. The leader does FIRST what he wants the other children to do.

So, the leader is to do his job first. That makes perfect sense because they are LEADERS, thus they should LEAD. In fact, per Merriam-Webster Dictionary, the definition of the word lead is:

1. a: to guide on a way especially by going in advance
   b: to direct on a course or in a direction
   c: to serve as a channel for <a pipe leads water to the house> to go through: live <lead a quiet life>

2. a: (1) to direct the operations, activity, or performance of <lead an orchestra> (2): to have charge of <lead a campaign
: (1): to go at the head of <lead a parade> (2): to be first in or among <lead the league> (3): to have a margin over <led his opponent>

So, every one of these definitions of the word lead insinuate that the person that does the leading should be doing the thing they do to lead FIRST, before the people that follow do their part. So, if that is the case then why do we turn this around when it comes to Biblical relationships? Why do we expect the people that follow to do their part first?

Consequently, in a marriage relationship, if the husband is to be the leader then he should "love his wife as Christ loved the Church" BEFORE he expects his wife to submit to him. In a parent/child relationship, if the father is the leader then he should "not provoke them to wrath and bring them up in the training and admonition of the Lord" BEFORE the children should be expected to obey their father.

Well, if the Church is to be based on relationships and relationships have two sides then what are those two sides?

Hebrews 13:17 "Obey those who rule over you, and be submissive, for they watch out for your souls, as those who must give account. Let them do so with joy and not with grief, for that would be unprofitable for you."

This verse gives both sides of the Church relationship. The people are to submit to the leadership BECAUSE the leadership watches out for their souls. I saw this over six years ago, just after my husband died and I started asking every Pastor I knew this question. What does it mean to you in very practical ways to watch out for your people's souls and can you back your answer up with Scripture? I was shocked at the responses I received. The first Pastor I asked got angry and walked away from me.

Some of the Pastors I would ask would try to answer this question but they all seemed to be incomplete answers to me. One Pastor answered this question with this Scripture:

Ezekiel 33:1-6 "Again the word of the Lord came to me, saying, 2 "Son of man, speak to the children of your people, and say to them: 'When I bring the sword upon a land, and the people of the land take a man from their territory and make him their watchman, 3 when he sees the sword coming upon the land, if he blows the trumpet and warns the people, 4 then whoever hears the sound of the trumpet and does not

take warning, if the sword comes and takes him away, his blood shall be on his own head. 5 He heard the sound of the trumpet, but did not take warning; his blood shall be upon himself. But he who takes warning will save his life. 6 But if the watchman sees the sword coming and does not blow the trumpet, and the people are not warned, and the sword comes and takes any person from among them, he is taken away in his iniquity; but his blood I will require at the watchman's hand.'"

He told me, "I see 'watching out for my people's souls' as being a watchman and warning them when danger is coming." I left his office and had to think about his answer for a while but as I was thinking about it, I felt like this was not a complete answer. The reason this did not feel right to me is because I knew that the word Pastor meant to be a shepherd and I did not think a shepherd's responsibility was just to call out a warning and then let the sheep fend for themselves. In fact, when David was shepherd boy and a bear or lion came to threaten his flock, he did much more than just call out a warning, he actively protected his flock by killing the bear and the lion.

1 Samuel 17:34-35 "But David said to Saul, "Your servant used to keep his father's sheep, and when a lion or a bear came and took a lamb out of the flock, 35 I went out after it and struck it, and delivered the lamb from its mouth; and when it arose against me, I caught it by its beard, and struck and killed it."

Other Pastors have given me even less complete answers then that or they have ignored the question and politely ended the conversation with me. I did not even hear them admit that they did not know the answer. I would have loved to hear a Pastor admit that they did not know the answer to that question. Not because I wanted to gloat and lord it over them that I knew something they didn't, but because if they were humble enough to admit that they did not know the answer then that Pastor would be humble enough to admit when they were wrong and they would be willing to try to fix their mistakes. I would gladly serve a humble Pastor. But I did not hear that answer or an answer that felt complete to me in any way and it has left me feeling flabbergasted. If the Pastors don't know their part of the Church relationship, then how can they be doing it? If they are not doing their part, then how can they expect the people to do their part?

Imagine children playing on a teeter-totter. The teeter-totter symbolizes relationships. In the Church relationship, one child is the congregation and the other child is the Pastoral leadership staff. Both sides must work together for a teeter-totter to work or to be any fun to play on. If you take one of the children off the teeter-totter, then it is unbalanced and the teeter-totter won't work. The same thing happens in a relationship, whether that is a marriage relationship, a child/parent relationship, or a Church relationship. When relationships don't work, people get hurt.

Amy Leigh Moore

Chapter 3

Church Hurt

We can see that the Church relationship is not working by the number of people that have been hurt in the Church. Per the Barna Group, in 2010, close to 20 million Christians had left the Church because of Church Hurt. That was seven years ago, and I doubt if there has been much improvement in the past seven years. Church hurt is at epidemic proportions yet not very many Pastors are trying to find a cure for this epidemic. In fact, I have seen the exact opposite reaction to Church hurt than trying to fix the problem. Most Pastors either bury their heads in the sand and pretend the problem is not as bad as it is or they blame the people that got hurt for their own hurt. But pretending the problem does not exist or blaming the victims will not fix the problem. This problem will not fix itself and I doubt if it is going anywhere any time soon.

I had a counselor tell this to me many years ago; he said, "With more authority automatically come more responsibility. If the people in authority do not fulfill the responsibility, then that is abuse. Plain and simple." I believe that is rampant in our Churches. Pastors do not understand what the responsibility is that comes with the authority of their position, so they are abusing the people they have authority over. Then we wonder why Church hurt is at epidemic proportions.

I have personal experience with very deep Church hurt. I was widowed in 2011. My husband, Dean, was my best friend and I loved him deeply. He was a man of unconditional love and he had a very soft heart. The only problem was that the heart that would accept people unconditionally was also riddled with heart disease. He had a five-way bypass performed in 1999, before we started dating, at the age of 28. We married in 2002 and in 2005 the heart disease reared its ugly head again. Between 2005 and 2011, when he died, he had twelve stents placed in his heart and his third heart attack is what killed him. We were in the hospital ER more times than I can count! Yet through all this I had to handle it all alone. We had moved to Tulsa so that

I could attend Oral Roberts University and we had no family there so I was hoping that the Church would be my family. Even when I begged for a Pastor or someone from the Church to be there at the hospital with me, I was left all alone. This happened multiple times in different Churches. It was not just a onetime event nor was it just one Church that hurt me.

There was one time that really stands out to me. Dean ended up in the hospital again with chest pains in 2010. The Doctors decided to do another heart catheter on him. A heart catheter is a small camera that is inserted into the heart through one of the major arteries. It is a common procedure but can still be a dangerous procedure because they are inserting a foreign object into the heart. The Doctors can see any blockages by using the camera and then they can use a balloon to open the blockage up and insert a stent if they need to. The stent is a small metal tube that holds the artery open.

I was so stressed out that I was in a bit of a panic. I was a Theology major at Oral Roberts University and thus I had a friend at school who had already been in ministry and called herself a Pastor. I called her, hoping that she would be willing to come and sit with me in the hospital while Dean was going through the procedure.

She told me, "Oh I wish I could but I am in the grocery store right now. You know I have absolutely no food in the house." I was hurt and angry. Her grocery shopping was more important than I and my husband were to her. The grocery store would have still been there after we got out of the hospital.

My last experience with Church hurt was the worst one. Two weeks after Dean died, I received a letter from the Social Security Administration. They informed me that the disability payments were being discontinued because I was not disabled and my husband, who was disabled, was now deceased. This was my only source of income because I was full time student at ORU and now I was losing that. I was still reeling from the loss of my husband and now I had been given a double blow. I no longer had any income.

I needed love and Spiritual support at that time and I felt like that kind of support should be available in the Church. I was not even considering financial support because I was too overwhelmed with grief to even think about money at that time! I needed a shoulder to cry on.

So, I tried to get an appointment with the same Pastor that performed my husband's memorial service. We had become members of his Church only a month earlier. I could not make an appointment with him because I think he was out of town.

Chapter 3: Church Hurt

So, I wrote him a letter. I poured my heart out in that letter and all my grief and sadness was in that letter. I remember crying my eyes out as I wrote it. I dropped it off to the Church and I felt as if he would help me.

A while later, I received a letter in return. I was kind of surprised to get a letter from him; why not just call me or invite me into his office? He knew my phone number because we had to give that information when we became members of the church. His letter said that he felt I needed healing and that he recommended a "Healing Week" at his Church. I looked the Healing Week up on the Church's website and found out that the cost of this "Healing Week" was $1000. I was shocked and incredulous! How could a Pastor who knew I had no income recommend a "Healing Week" that cost $1000 and not offer to pay any of the cost for me? Who was he serving; God or money?

I wrote another letter to him and asked him these exact questions. I wanted to make sure that the Senior Pastor received this letter personally so I sent it to him as a registered letter that required his signature to be received. I was not sure if the first letter had been sent by the Senior Pastor or a secretary or an Assistant Pastor and I did not want to wrongly accuse him of serving money instead of God if this did not come directly from him.

I was sent the receipt with his signature on it from the Post Office so I knew he had personally received this letter. I received a reply within a few days. He asked me to not contact him anymore and he made it very clear that I would no longer be welcome in his Church. I was so upset that I tossed the letter. So, on top of the grief of losing my husband, I also had another Church rejection to deal with. My only regret is that I did not keep his letters.

It was after these experiences that I left the Church and started asking God what was wrong with the Church. That summer God showed me Hebrews 13:17 and I started asking Pastors the question of what it means to them to "watch out for the souls" of their people. I soon realized that Pastors do not know what that means so there is no way they can be doing it. If they are not doing their part in the Church relationship then it is no wonder so many people, including myself have been deeply hurt in the church.

So, what exactly is Church hurt? The first step in fixing the problem is to identify it. This is the definition of Church hurt that a friend of mine came up with and I think it is perfect. "Church hurt happens when Pastors intentionally or unintentionally neglect the physical, spiritual, and psychological needs of the people." This definition is as complete of a definition as I can imagine.

Why does Church hurt happen? There are millions of reasons Church hurt happens. Probably a different reason for every story of Church hurt out there. But I have chosen four reasons that seem to be the most prevalent to me.

I believe the first reason that Church hurt happens is because of a lack of knowledge on the part of the leadership.

Hosea 4:6 "My people are destroyed for lack of knowledge. Because you have rejected knowledge, I also will reject you from being priest for Me; because you have forgotten the law of your God, I also will forget your children."

Most Christians can quote from memory the first part of this verse but the second part is even more important. This must start with the leadership. Notice that God will reject the Priests (Church leaders) if they reject God's knowledge. If the priests reject God's knowledge, then God will reject them and their children. Many Church leaders have rejected God's knowledge about leadership and thus have put themselves in the position to receive the consequences from the second half of this verse. Not because they purposely are doing it but because they don't know any better. That is such a shame because as a Pastor or Church Leader they should know better and don't. That lack of knowledge will hurt and destroy people. God is a patient God but He will only allow His people to be hurt for so long before He does something.

The second reason is putting rules and regulations ahead of compassion and care, especially in our benevolence ministries. This happened to Dean and me not long after we had moved to Tulsa. We moved to Tulsa in July of 2008 and in August of that year I started school at ORU. At first everything went just fine. We started attending one of the largest Churches in Tulsa and I loved school. We lived off Dean's Social Security Disability of $700 a month and we also qualified for food stamps. We had enough to get by and I could complete my education.

Then in December of 2008, we received a knock on our door. I answered it and a woman stood outside the door and she handed me her card. She said, "The owner of this complex has gone into foreclosure, I am from the bank and it is my job to let you know that you have 30 days to vacate the property."

I had no idea what to do or where to go. We only had Dean's disability check for income which meant we did not have enough money for deposits and the like for a new apartment. I was not even sure if this was legal so I did some checking and I found out that it was all perfectly legal. We had a lease and our rent was paid in full but because

Chapter 3: Church Hurt

the owner went into foreclosure the lease was invalid and the bank had every right to evict us.

So now what? We had spent all our money to move to Tulsa and $700 a month was not much to move on. I tried to call the school but they did not have housing for married couples so there was nothing they could do to help. Since we had no family here in Tulsa, I called the only other place I could think of to call; the large Church we had joined when we moved here.

We went and filled out the paperwork for help from the Church. We needed $750 for the first month rent plus the deposit of another apartment that we found. We thought for sure they would help us out. They were one of the largest Churches in town and we felt $750 would just be a drop in the bucket for them. Without talking with us or confirming anything we told them, they gave us a grand total of $100. They did not care enough about us to sit down and talk with us or to delve deeper into our circumstances. They didn't even offer to get people together to help us move or call us to follow up on our situation. I felt like I had been punched in the gut! How could they turn us away like that?

God did provide in another way and we got moved and the ORU Missions and Outreach Department sent a bunch of kids over to help us get moved. We had about 15 volunteers so it only took a couple of hours to get us moved into the new apartment. But that did not negate the hurt I felt when the Church refused to help us.

If we put rules and regulations ahead of compassion and care, then we are just like the world. The Church we were in, put rules and regulations ahead of compassion and care.

Have you ever had to go to the welfare office to ask for Government help? I had to when Dean became sick and could no longer work. It was a very demeaning process because the system saw us as a case number instead of as people that were dealing with difficult situations. I have nothing against social workers. I know they are only doing their job but the social service industry has taught them not to get emotionally involved in their cases. In other words, do not love the people you are trying to help.

That attitude has seeped into our Church benevolence ministries as well and even though these people may be very well intentioned, giving people financial help without giving them love is not what God intended at all. Many Church benevolence ministries only give small amounts of money to hurting people without giving any true care or compassion.

Matthew 22:39 "And the second is like it: 'You shall love your neighbor as yourself.'"

Now this does not mean that rules are not necessary. I understand that we need to have certain rules in place or people will abuse the generosity of God's people. But love needs to supersede the rules. The rules cannot define everyone's situation. We need to have love to be able to look past the surface and see what people really need. One of my favorite quotes is this: "Obedience keeps the rules. Love knows when to break them." by Anthony de Mello. This quote sums this reason up perfectly. When we put rules before love, people get hurt.

The third reason Church hurt happens is that we judge by appearances. This is the reason I experienced the Church hurt that I experienced. Dean had heart disease and heart disease is an invisible disease. That means that it cannot be seen by just looking at a person. When people looked at him they saw a healthy thirty-something man. They judged him as lazy because he was not working. But what they did not see, because they did not take the time nor did they care enough to see, was a man whose heart was riddled with disease. He died at age forty but his doctor told him he had a heart of an eighty-year-old man.

John 7:24 "Do not judge according to appearance, but judge with righteous judgment."

Jesus told us that we need to judge with a righteous judgment and to stop judging by appearances. If Jesus told us to do it then it can be done because if Jesus told us to do something that could not be done, then He would be unjust and unfair. So how do we judge with a righteous judgment? Well, the first way we do this is to stop making assumptions about people. Another one of my favorites quotes comes from Oscar Wilde. He stated, "When you assume, you make an ass out of u and me." That is very true.

The second way to stop judging by appearances is to view people through the eyes of love. Only through the eyes of love can we judge with a righteous judgment. When we love a person, we want to get to know them and talk with them. So instead of assuming things about people and thus judging them by their appearance, we should talk with them and get to know them and find out what is going on in their lives.

The last reason Church hurt happens is that we put our rituals ahead of our relationships. As I stated earlier, ritual is not necessarily a bad thing but when that ritual is put ahead of relationship then it can hurt people.

Luke 5:17-25 *"Now it happened on a certain day, as He was teaching, that there were Pharisees and teachers of the law sitting by, who had come out of every town of Galilee, Judea, and Jerusalem. And the power of the Lord was present to heal them. Then behold, men brought on a bed a man who was paralyzed, whom they sought to bring in and lay before Him. And when they could not find how they might bring him in, because of the crowd, they went up on the housetop and let him down with his bed through the tiling into the midst before Jesus. When He saw their faith, He said to him, "Man, your sins are forgiven you." And the scribes and the Pharisees began to reason, saying, "Who is this who speaks blasphemies? Who can forgive sins but God alone?" But when Jesus perceived their thoughts, He answered and said to them, "Why are you reasoning in your hearts? Which is easier, to say, 'Your sins are forgiven you,' or to say, 'Rise up and walk'? But that you may know that the Son of Man has power on earth to forgive sins"—He said to the man who was paralyzed, "I say to you, arise, take up your bed, and go to your house." Immediately he rose up before them, took up what he had been lying on, and departed to his own house, glorifying God."*

There are two things I want you to see from this passage. First, notice that Jesus stopped his preaching to minister to this man and his friends. He put the needs of this man before the ritual of his teaching. Jesus understood that relationship should come before ritual. The second thing I want to point out is that Jesus never said a word about the hole in the roof. Jesus grew up as the Son of a carpenter so He probably went up there after everyone left and fixed the roof Himself. Would that happen in today's Church? Or would these men be sued for destruction of property? Jesus put other people's needs before His own need to finish His teaching and the ritual of a Church service. Shouldn't we be doing the same thing?

So how do we, in this time and in this culture, contain this epidemic of Church Hurt and start to preserve our society? This seems like an overwhelming job and too big for one Church or one Pastor to do. Well, it is a huge responsibility but I believe it is possible if we build the Church on a full foundation instead of a partial foundation.

Amy Leigh Moore

Chapter 4

The Cornerstone of the Church

Matthew 28:19-20 "Go therefore and make disciples of all the nations, baptizing them in the name of the Father and of the Son and of the Holy Spirit, teaching them to observe all things that I have commanded you; and lo, I am with you always, even to the end of the age." Amen."

Would you say this is the mission statement of the Church? I would. So, if this is the mission statement then I wonder how well we are doing it? I would say we have done well at "going" into all the world. Christianity is known in every corner of the world. I would say we have done well in baptizing them, as well. I would say we have even done a decent job of "teaching them to observe all the things that Christ commanded us". But how well have we done the job of making disciples? I think we need a lot of improvement when it comes to making disciples.

So how do we make disciples? Before we begin to answer that question, we must look at the foundation of the Church. Because if we do not have a complete foundation under the Church then however we answer that question will be incomplete and it will fall very short of what God intended.

So, what is the foundation of the Church supposed to look like? Well, it starts with the Cornerstone. Most people will say that Jesus is the foundation of the Church but I do not see that in Scripture. I see that Jesus is the Cornerstone, not the full foundation.

This is what the Church looks like when we try to make the Cornerstone into the full foundation.

Notice that when we try to make Jesus the full foundation there is a huge part of the Church that has no foundation. But that is exactly what most of the Church world has done. They have tried to make the Cornerstone into the full foundation. It sounds very righteous to say that Jesus is the foundation of the Church but it is not accurate. Scripture says that Jesus is the Cornerstone that all the rest of the foundation is built on.

> *Psalm 118:22 "The stone which the builders rejected has become the chief cornerstone."*

> *Matthew 21:42 "Jesus said to them, "Have you never read in the Scriptures: 'The stone which the builders rejected has become the chief cornerstone. This was the Lord's doing, and it is marvelous in our eyes'?"*

> *Mark 12:10 "Have you not even read this Scripture: 'The stone which the builders rejected has become the chief cornerstone."*

> *Luke 20:17 "Then He looked at them and said, "What then is this that is written: 'The stone which the builders rejected has become the chief cornerstone'*

> *Acts 4:11 "This is the 'stone which was rejected by you builders, which has become the chief cornerstone."*

1 Peter 2:6-7 "Therefore it is also contained in the Scripture, "Behold, I lay in Zion a chief cornerstone, elect, precious, and he who believes on Him will by no means be put to shame." Therefore, to you who believe, He is precious; but to those who are disobedient, "The stone which the builders rejected has become the chief cornerstone,"

So, what exactly is a cornerstone? This is the definition of a cornerstone from Merriam-Webster's Dictionary "1. stone forming a part of a corner or angle in a wall; specifically: such a stone laid at a formal ceremony. 2. a basic element"

To define a cornerstone even further, let's look at the Greek and Hebrew definitions of a cornerstone as well. Hebrew is the language that the Old Testament was written in and Greek is the language that the New Testament was written in. I always find it enlightening to look at the meanings of the original languages when I am studying the Bible.

The Greek word for Cornerstone is akrogóniaios which means "at the extreme angle or corner". The Hebrew word for Cornerstone is pinnah which means "bulwark, chief, corner, stay, tower". These definitions also imply that Jesus is the Cornerstone not the full foundation. So why has most of the Church world taught that Jesus is the foundation of the Church? I believe they have done this because it is easier than studying to find out what the full foundation of the Church is supposed to be.

"Therefore whoever hears these sayings of Mine, and does them, I will liken him to a wise man who built his house on the rock: 25 and the rain descended, the floods came, and the winds blew and beat on that house; and it did not fall, for it was founded on the rock. But everyone who hears these sayings of Mine, and does not do them, will be like a foolish man who built his house on the sand: 27 and the rain descended, the floods came, and the winds blew and beat on that house; and it fell. And great was its fall." Matthew 7:24-27

When we build on an incomplete foundation then when the storms come, the building will collapse, and when it collapses, it will hurt a lot of people that are within that building. Therefore, I am adamant about building on a complete foundation. If we build on a partial foundation, then more people will get hurt.

Amy Leigh Moore

Chapter 5

The Full Foundation of the Church

So, what is the full foundation of the Church supposed to be? Here is a picture of what I believe the foundation of the Church should look like.

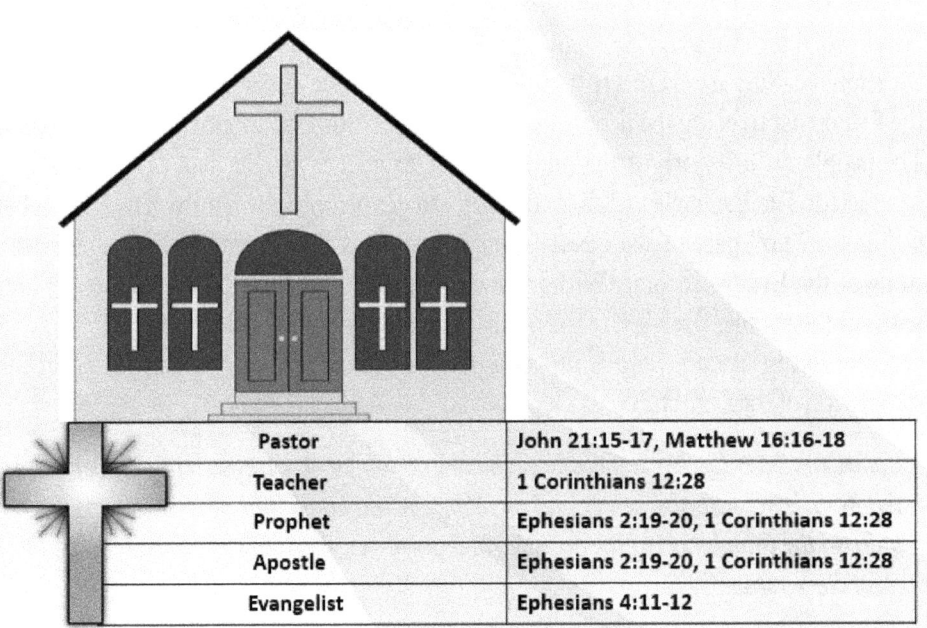

Pastor	John 21:15-17, Matthew 16:16-18
Teacher	1 Corinthians 12:28
Prophet	Ephesians 2:19-20, 1 Corinthians 12:28
Apostle	Ephesians 2:19-20, 1 Corinthians 12:28
Evangelist	Ephesians 4:11-12

I believe that the ministerial gifts are the foundation of the Church. Where I differ from Orthodox Religion is that I do not believe that the actual people who were the Apostles and the Prophets are the foundation of the Church. How can imperfect men be the correct foundation for a perfect Church? What happens when those people die?

Does the foundation of the Church crumble and die with those people? I believe that the Offices or Jobs of the Ministerial Gifts are the foundation of the Church.

So, what exactly is the jobs of the five-fold ministry gifts? If you will notice, I have added Scripture to each one of the ministerial gifts. I have also put these gifts in a specific order. There is a very good reason for the order I have used to build this foundation.

Jesus is the Cornerstone but how does the rest of the foundation fit with the Cornerstone? Well, I believe the first brick after Jesus in this foundation is the job of the Evangelist.

Ephesians 4:11-12 "And He Himself gave some to be apostles, some prophets, some evangelists, and some pastors and teachers, for the equipping of the saints for the work of ministry, for the edifying of the body of Christ"

Without the Evangelist than a lot fewer people would become born again. The Greek word for evangelist is euaggelistés – properly, an "evangelist"; someone with a vocational calling from God to announce the good news of the Gospel. We must have the Evangelist to bring the people into the family of God and to spread this good news. The people do the work of the ministry so without the people that work cannot be completed. The Evangelist's job is to bring the people into the family. The Evangelist fulfills the "go" part of the Great Commission. This is the reason I have placed the stone of the Evangelist first. Without the Evangelist, we do not have the people and without the people, the work of the ministry cannot be completed.

The next brick to be laid is the Apostle. The Apostle is an important brick in the foundation of the Church.

Ephesians 2:19-20 "Now, therefore, you are no longer strangers and foreigners, but fellow citizens with the saints and members of the household of God, having been built on the foundation of the apostles and prophets, Jesus Christ Himself being the chief cornerstone"

1 Corinthians 12:28 "And God has appointed these in the church: first apostles, second prophets, third teachers, after that miracles, then gifts of healings, helps, administrations, varieties of tongues."

Notice that the Apostle was the first gift given in 1 Corinthians 12:28 and the Apostle is called the foundation in Ephesians 2:19-20. So, what is the definition of an

Apostle? From HELPS Word-studies: apóstolos – properly, someone sent (commissioned), focusing back on the authority (commissioning) of the sender; apostle. So, an Apostle is sent but sent to do what?

By studying the ministry of Paul, I have developed my own definition of an Apostle. My definition of an Apostle is a person that God anoints to start new ministries. Paul started new ministries and would train the leaders like Timothy and then he would move on. I believe that is still the job of the Apostle because we will always need new ministries started to complete the work of the Church. The Apostle also fulfills the "go" part of the Great Commission and he starts the discipleship process by planting the seeds of discipleship. The Apostle is a vital part of the foundation of the Church because without the Apostle our ministries would become old and stagnate. That is why I have placed the Apostle as the second level in the foundation of the Church.

The next brick in this foundation is the Prophet. The Prophet also has an important role to play in the foundation of the Church.

Ephesians 2:19-20 "Now, therefore, you are no longer strangers and foreigners, but fellow citizens with the saints and members of the household of God, having been built on the foundation of the apostles and prophets, Jesus Christ Himself being the chief cornerstone"

1 Corinthians 12:28 "And God has appointed these in the church: first apostles, second prophets, third teachers, after that miracles, then gifts of healings, helps, administrations, varieties of tongues."

Notice that Ephesians 2:19-20 says that the Prophet is part of the foundation of the Church and 1 Corinthians 12:28 says that the Prophet was the second gift that was given. The foundation must be laid before the rest of the building can be built so that is why the Prophet is part of the foundation of the Church.

So, what exactly is the job of the Prophet? From HELPS Word-studies: prophḗtēs – properly, one who speaks forth by the inspiration of God; a prophet. A prophet declares the mind (message) of God, which sometimes predicts the future (foretelling) – and more commonly, speaks forth His message for a situation. A Prophet then is someone inspired by God to foretell or tell-forth (forthtell) the Word of God.

The prophet also brings correction when necessary. When David had sinned with Bathsheba, God sent Nathan the Prophet to confront David with that sin. God uses His Prophets to bring correction to us when we miss the mark.

2 Samuel 12:1-15 "Then the Lord sent Nathan to David. And he came to him, and said to him: "There were two men in one city, one rich and the other poor. [2] The rich man had exceedingly many flocks and herds. [3] But the poor man had nothing, except one little ewe lamb which he had bought and nourished; and it grew up together with him and with his children. It ate of his own food and drank from his own cup and lay in his bosom; and it was like a daughter to him. [4] And a traveler came to the rich man, who refused to take from his own flock and from his own herd to prepare one for the wayfaring man who had come to him; but he took the poor man's lamb and prepared it for the man who had come to him." [5] So David's anger was greatly aroused against the man, and he said to Nathan, "As the Lord lives, the man who has done this shall surely die! [6] And he shall restore fourfold for the lamb, because he did this thing and because he had no pity." [7] Then Nathan said to David, "You are the man! Thus says the Lord God of Israel: 'I anointed you king over Israel, and I delivered you from the hand of Saul. [8] I gave you your master's house and your master's wives into your keeping, and gave you the house of Israel and Judah. And if that had been too little, I also would have given you much more! [9] Why have you despised the commandment of the Lord, to do evil in His sight? You have killed Uriah the Hittite with the sword; you have taken his wife to be your wife, and have killed him with the sword of the people of Ammon. [10] Now therefore, the sword shall never depart from your house, because you have despised Me, and have taken the wife of Uriah the Hittite to be your wife.' [11] Thus says the Lord: 'Behold, I will raise up adversity against you from your own house; and I will take your wives before your eyes and give them to your neighbor, and he shall lie with your wives in the sight of this sun. [12] For you did it secretly, but I will do this thing before all Israel, before the sun.'" [13] So David said to Nathan, "I have sinned against the Lord." And Nathan said to David, "The Lord also has put away your sin; you shall not die. [14] However, because by this deed you have given great occasion to the enemies of the Lord to blaspheme, the child also who is born to you shall surely die." [15] Then Nathan departed to his house."

The Prophet fulfills part of the "teaching them to observe all things that I have commanded you" in the Great Commission along with the Teacher. We must be careful when listening to a Prophet, however. There are many false prophets out there so we need to have some sort of criteria in which to know whether a Prophet is from God. That criterion is does the word the Prophet bring agree with the Written Word or not? If what a Prophet says does not agree with the Written Word of God, then that Prophet is not from God. This means we must know the Scriptures for ourselves and not rely on what other people tell us the Bible says.

The fourth layer in the foundation of the Church is that of the Teacher. The Teacher fulfills a vital function in the foundation of the Church.

1 Corinthians 12:28 "And God has appointed these in the church: first apostles, second prophets, third teachers, after that miracles, then gifts of healings, helps, administrations, varieties of tongues."

Notice that the Teacher is the third gift given in 1 Corinthians 12:28. This is because the Teacher is part of the foundation of the Church and is necessary to that foundation to teach the people to do the work of the ministry.

So, what is the definition of the Teacher? From HELPS Word-studies: didáskō (from daō, "learn") – to teach (literally, "cause to learn"); instruct, impart knowledge (disseminate information). In the NT, didáskō ("teach") nearly always refers to teaching the Scriptures (the written Word of God). The key role of teaching Scripture is shown by its great frequency in the NT, and the variety of word-forms.

The Teacher completes the "teaching them to observe all things that I have commanded you" in the Great Commission. Without the teacher, this part of the Great Commission would be impossible.

The last layer in the foundation of the Church is that of the Pastor. Next to Jesus as the Cornerstone, I believe the Pastor is the second most vital part of the foundation. The Pastor is closest to the people and is the connection between the people and the rest of the foundation. To this end, the Pastor will be discussed separately.

Amy Leigh Moore

Chapter 6

The Pastor

Before we start to discuss the job of the Pastor, I would like to ask a question. How do we make disciples?

***Matthew 28:19-20** "Go therefore and make disciples of all the nations, baptizing them in the name of the Father and of the Son and of the Holy Spirit, teaching them to observe all things that I have commanded you; and lo, I am with you always, even to the end of the age." Amen."*

Jesus commands us to "make disciples" but how do we do this? To help answer this question let's look at the Greek meaning of the phrase "make disciples". From HELPS Word-studies the phrase "make disciples" means: "mathēteúō – to disciple, i.e. helping someone to progressively learn the Word of God to become a matured, growing disciple (literally, "a learner," a true Christ-follower); to train (develop) in the truths of Scripture and the lifestyle required, i.e. helping a believer learn to be a disciple of Christ in belief and practice."

This definition is much more involved than just Salvation. This definition implies a long-term relationship. Jesus even demonstrated how to make disciples. He spent almost 24 hours a day, 7 days a week for three years with the 12 men He chose to be His disciples. He walked with them and talked with them. He ate with them and slept with them. He put up with their squabbling and taught them how to love one another. That is how we make disciples.

Let me ask you another question. Is Salvation the first step in that discipleship process?

***John 20:19-23** "Then, the same day at evening, being the first day of the week, when the doors were shut where the disciples were assembled, for fear of the Jews, Jesus came and stood in the midst, and said to them, "Peace be with you." When He had* *said this, He showed them His hands and His side. Then the disciples were glad when they saw the Lord. So Jesus said to them again, "Peace to you! As the Father has sent Me, I also send you." And when He had said this, He breathed on them, and said to them, "Receive the Holy Spirit. If you forgive the sins of any, they are forgiven them; if you retain the sins of any, they are retained."*

This was when the disciples became born again. Notice that this happened AFTER Jesus died and rose again and AFTER He had discipled these men for three years. If Salvation was the first step in the discipleship process then Jesus would have died on the cross, rose from the dead, and THEN started His ministry and discipled these men. Instead He came to earth discipled these men and THEN died and rose again.

Yet, in most of our Churches we stress getting "saved". Now I am not saying that becoming born again is not important. But salvation is only one step in the process of "making disciples" and it may not even be the first step in the process. I believe the first step in the process of making disciples is to unconditionally love people just as Jesus unconditionally loved His disciples. Disciples are made by showing the type of sacrificial love in relationships that Jesus demonstrated and teaching others to do the same. Since most Churches stress salvation, I wonder if we are truly making disciples or are we making converts?

The Pastor has the key role in making disciples. So, what exactly is the definition of the Pastor? From HELPS Word-studies: "poimén – properly, a shepherd ("pastor" in Latin); someone who the Lord raises up to care for the total well-being of His flock (the people of the Lord)". This definition tells us that a Pastor's responsibility is to care for the TOTAL well-being of the people. This includes but is not just limited to the Spiritual well-being of the people.

The Pastor fulfills the "making disciples" part of the Great Commission by developing relationships with the people and loving them with a sacrificial love that meets ALL their needs, like a shepherd meets the needs of his flock.

Now this does not mean they must meet all the flock's needs personally. They are responsible to meet the people's needs just as a CEO is responsible to make sure a company is profitable and stays in business. The CEO of a company does not personally do EVERY job necessary for a company to meet its goals but he is responsible for all those jobs. If the accountant is not doing his job correctly, the CEO has a responsibility to either retrain the accountant or find a new one. I heard someone say this the other day and it is excellent so I am using it: leaders can delegate jobs but they cannot delegate responsibility. A Pastor may not have to personally do everything required to care for the total well-be of the people but he is responsible to make sure all their needs are met.

I believe this is what the disciples did that we are not doing and therefore we do not see the same type of anointing and power that the disciples saw in the book of Acts.

John 21:15-17 "So when they had eaten breakfast, Jesus said to Simon Peter, "Simon, son of Jonah, do you love Me more than these?" He said to Him, "Yes, Lord; You know that I love You." He said to him, "Feed My lambs." He said to him again a second time, "Simon, son of Jonah, do you love Me?" He said to Him, "Yes, Lord; You know that I love You." He said to him, "Tend My sheep." He said to him the third time, "Simon, son of Jonah, do you love Me?" Peter was grieved because He said to him the third time, "Do you love Me?" And he said to Him, "Lord, You know all things; You know that I love You." Jesus said to him, "Feed My sheep."

Jesus was doing more than just reinstating Peter in John 21:15-17. He was handing the Shepherding baton off to Peter and consequently any other Pastor that followed Peter. How do I know this? Jesus used the language of a Shepherd. He did not have to use that language but he deliberately used the language of a Shepherd. Jesus was not a man to use frivolous language so we can be sure that if he used a certain type of language He meant what He said. Jesus was using the language of a Shepherd to communicate that Peter was to take care of the people in the same way a real shepherd cares for sheep. Jesus is the Good Shepherd but He was telling Peter that he was to be an under-shepherd. God works through people so once Jesus ascended to Heaven, He needed other people to be His hands and feet and be shepherds for the people on earth.

Here is one more Scripture that can confirm this claim that a Pastor is to care for the people as a literal Shepherd and not just as a Spiritual Shepherd.

Acts 20:28 "Therefore take heed to yourselves and to all the flock, among which the Holy Spirit has made you overseers, to shepherd the church of God which He purchased with His own blood."

The following quote tells us what a literal shepherd's job was. "In early morning, he led forth the flock from the fold, marching at its head to the spot where they were to be pastured. Here he watched them all day, taking care that none of the sheep strayed, and if any for a time eluded his watch and wandered away from the rest, seeking diligently till he found and brought it back. In those lands sheep require to be supplied regularly with water, and the shepherd for this purpose has to guide them either to some running stream or to wells dug in the wilderness and furnished with troughs. At night, he brought the flock home to the fold, counting them as they passed under the rod at the door to assure himself that none were missing. Nor did his labors always end with sunset. Often, he had to guard the fold through the dark hours from the attack of wild beasts, or the wily attempts of the prowling thief."

Notice that the shepherd is in front of the flock, not to lord it over them but to lead them to good pastures, just as the game "follow the leader" illustrated. The shepherd watched over the sheep ALL DAY and diligently went after those that had gone astray.

The shepherd goes after the sheep. He does not expect the sheep to come to him. Yet in today's Church we tell the people to come to the Church. The shepherd no longer goes to the people.

The shepherd took care of their physical needs by giving them good pasture to graze on (food) and he supplied them with water and housing at night. Most Churches do a pretty god job on the food and water. But how many of them are providing housing for the poor?

The shepherd took care of the sheep's safety needs by staying with them and guarding them against thieves. We have an epidemic of Church hurt in this country so how can the Pastors or shepherds be keeping us safe? What would our Churches look like if our Pastors were this kind of shepherd?

Here are some Scriptures on being a good shepherd.

Psalm 23:1-2 *"The LORD is my shepherd; I shall not want. He makes me to lie down in green pastures; He leads me beside the still waters."*

Since Jesus handed off the baton of being a good shepherd to Peter and thus to every other Pastor that came after him then this verse not only describes what the Lord will do but also describes what our earthly shepherds should be doing as well. Does this mean they will do it perfectly like God does? Not at all! And I do not expect them to do it perfectly; but this is what they should be striving toward and if they mess up then they need to admit their mistake and repent and try to fix that mistake. If our Pastors would try to be this type of shepherd, then God's grace and mercy will fill in their weak spots.

Matthew 18:12-13 *""What do you think? If a man has a hundred sheep, and one of them goes astray, does he not leave the ninety-nine and go to the mountains to seek*

the one that is straying? And if he should find it, assuredly, I say to you, he rejoices more over that sheep than over the ninety-nine that did not go astray."

Instead of actively pursuing the sheep that have gone astray, most Pastors have tried to lure the sheep back to the Church. But this is not what this verse says to do. This verse says that the shepherd leaves those that are safe and actively pursues the one that has gone astray. Does the Pastor do this personally? Not at all! But he should have a team that will actively call those that have left the Church, find out why they left and try to fix the reason they left.

Jeremiah 33:12-13 "Thus says the Lord of hosts: 'In this place which is desolate, without man and without beast, and in all its cities, there shall again be a dwelling place of shepherds causing their flocks to lie down. In the cities of the mountains, in the cities of the lowland, in the cities of the South, in the land of Benjamin, in the places around Jerusalem, and in the cities of Judah, the flocks shall again pass under the hands of him who counts them,' says the Lord."

The Church should be the place where people could lie down and sleep because they feel safe and protected. But in most of our Churches people must pretend that their lives are perfect so they will not feel judged. How is that making people feel safe?

I Samuel 17:34-35 "But David said to Saul, "Your servant used to keep his father's sheep, and when a lion or a bear came and took a lamb out of the flock, I went out after it and struck it, and delivered the lamb from its mouth; and when it arose against me, I caught it by its beard, and struck and killed it."

The responsibility of the shepherd is to actively protect the flock. But many of our Pastors are failing in this job. When I was a child, my step-father sexually molested me and my two sisters. My mother found out about it and she did not know what to do about it so she went to the Pastor looking for guidance. The Pastor used these verses to advise my mom.

1 Peter 3:1-2 "Wives, likewise, be submissive to your own husbands, that even if some do not obey the word, they, without a word, may be won by the conduct of their wives, when they observe your chaste conduct accompanied by fear."

He advised my mom to stay in her marriage and believe that God would change her husband through that submission. Consequently, I was molested once and my sisters were molested many times. This Pastor and my mother failed to protect us. Both did not understand that the responsibility of the shepherd and the responsibility of a mother is to protect the children. It took a major scandal in the Catholic Church for laws to be passed that require Clergy to report child sexual abuse.

Per the child welfare guidelines for the US, "Approximately 27 States and Guam currently include members of the clergy among those professionals specifically mandated by law to report known or suspected instances of child abuse or neglect. In approximately 18 States and Puerto Rico, any person who suspects child abuse or neglect is required to report it. This inclusive language appears to include clergy but may be interpreted otherwise".

What a shame that it took our Government to pass laws that require Clergy to report child sexual abuse before it was done. How can Pastors call themselves shepherds if they are not protecting the children in their Church?

So, how do Pastors fulfill the responsibility of being a good shepherd in today's world? Well, the Bible gives us that answer.

Isaiah 58:6-7 ""Is this not the fast that I have chosen: to loose the bonds of wickedness, to undo the heavy burdens, to let the oppressed go free, and that you break every yoke? Is it not to share your bread with the hungry, and that you bring to your house the poor who are cast out; when you see the naked, that you cover him, and not hide yourself from your own flesh?"

The Pastor of the Church that only gave us $100 when we needed $750 to move because the owner of our apartment complex got foreclosed on and the bank was kicking us out, was talking about how his Church did these verses instead of just talking about them. As he was talking about how well his Church does regarding these things, I could not help but wonder how he could make these claims when they virtually turned us away when we were being evicted out of our residence. Verse 7 says that "you bring to your house the poor who are cast out" yet when we were cast out no one offered to bring us into their home or even really help us to get our own home.

I found out later that their benevolence program has in writing that they will not help with rent or deposits. The money they did give us was the amount the apartment complex would accept to hold the apartment, not move us in. How can this Church claim to help with housing when they state in writing that they will not help with rent or deposits?

Chapter 6: The Pastor

A couple of years later I had the chance to confront this Pastor on this issue and I was told that they must state that in their paperwork to protect themselves. Well that goes against what the above Scripture says. Look at verse 8.

Isaiah 58:8 *"Then your light shall break forth like the morning, Your healing shall spring forth speedily, And your righteousness shall go before you; The glory of the Lord shall be your rear guard."*

So, God promises to be our rear guard or our protection when we do what these verses tell us to do. This Church obviously did not fully believe what God said or they would not have literally put into writing that they would not help with rents or deposits.

I was talking to a friend at school about what happened not long after I talked to this Pastor and she showed me something I will never forget.

She told me, "Amy stand up and put your hands on your butt."

I looked at her quizzically but did as she asked. I stood up and placed my hands on my butt. Then she asked me, "Without taking your hands off your butt, could you please pass me that bottle of water that is sitting on the table?"

Of course, I could not do so very easily and then she said something that blew my mind. (Excuse the language) "When we are protecting our own asses then we cannot serve other people the way we are supposed to serve them!"

This Church was more concerned about protecting themselves then they were truly helping other people. Now this is not to say that the Church should not be wise when dealing with other people. There are going to be people that try to use and abuse the Church but the Church should not disobey God's Word while trying to protect themselves.

There could have been other ways they could have protected themselves. This Church also had a job search ministry and they could make it a requirement for people who need help with housing to register with their job search ministry for those that can work. They could have also asked for doctor verification about my husband's illness. Any person that is truly disabled should have no problem showing doctor verification of their disability. The bottom line is that the Church did not care enough about us to look beyond the surface to see what the real problem was.

This Pastor did apologize and ask for forgiveness, which I gladly gave, but true repentance is about change as much as it is about remorse. This Pastor felt remorse about how we were treated but was not willing to change the policy so it was not true repentance. I could not stay and submit to a Pastor that was not truly repentant.

In Isaiah 58, God is redefining a fast here. These verses are not about abstaining from food. In fact, the Israelites had been abstaining from food but not seeing any results.

> *Isaiah 58:3-4 "'Why have we fasted,' they say, 'and You have not seen? Why have we afflicted our souls, and You take no notice?' "In fact, in the day of your fast you find pleasure, And exploit all your laborers. Indeed, you fast for strife and debate, And to strike with the fist of wickedness. You will not fast as you do this day, To make your voice heard on high."*

To be a shepherd in today's world is not much different than a shepherd in Bible times. The shepherd took care of all the needs of the sheep and we are to take care of all the needs of the people. God is telling the Israelites that the fast that He would prefer they do is to care for ALL the needs of the people.

Chapter 7

The Needs of the People

Let's look again at the Greek definition of the word Pastor - Poimēn – "properly, a shepherd ("pastor" in Latin); someone who the Lord raises up to care for the TOTAL WELL-BEING of His flock (the people of the Lord)." What does the TOTAL well-being of the people mean? Another way to say this is that the responsibility of the Pastor is to care for ALL the needs of the people. So, what are the needs of the people?

The most concise and effective tool to sum up the needs of the people that I have found is Maslow's Hierarchy of needs.

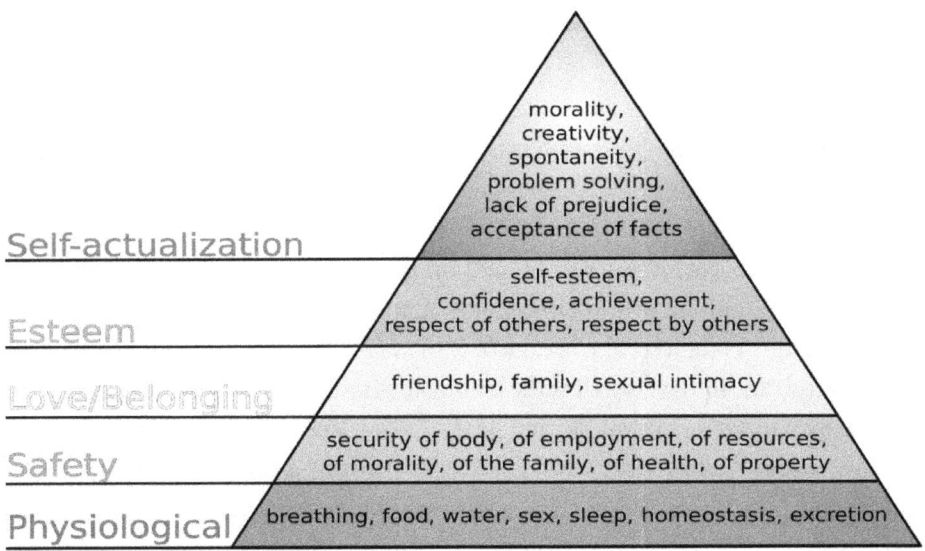

Most people have heard of Maslow's Hierarchy of Needs. Maslow wanted to understand what motivates people. He believed that people possess a set of motivation systems unrelated to rewards or unconscious desires. Maslow (1943) stated that people are motivated to achieve certain needs. When one need is fulfilled a person seeks to fulfill the next one, and so on. The earliest and most widespread version of Maslow's (1943, 1954) hierarchy of needs includes five motivational needs, often depicted as hierarchical levels within a pyramid. This five-stage model can be divided into basic (or deficiency) needs (e.g. physiological, safety, love, and esteem) and growth needs (self-actualization).

I am not using Maslow's Hierarchy of Needs in the same way that Maslow designed it. I am using his Hierarchy to illustrate what the needs of the people are and to give the Church leaders a viable tool to help meet those needs. Maslow's Hierarchy is not in the Bible but I believe the concept is Biblical.

So, let's look at each level of Maslow's Hierarchy individually. Physiological needs are our physical needs such as food, clothing, housing, transportation, and communication. These are the first needs that must be met for survival. If these needs are not met, then a person cannot even consider their other needs. Many Churches provide help with food and clothing needs through food banks and clothing banks but not nearly as many Churches provide for housing needs for the poor. Although this is starting to change a bit since the housing bubble burst in 2008 and left many families homeless. Food and clothing banks are good but they do not make any difference if a person does not have a kitchen in which to store and prepare the food or they do not have a closet in which to put the clothes away in.

So, why do Churches focus so much on food and clothing banks and so little on housing? The answer is in the costs associated with these different types of services. Food and clothing banks are virtually costless to the Church. Think about it; the food is usually donated from grocery stores and the clothes are donated from people in the community. Most of the time volunteers sort and clean the clothes as well as organize the food pantry. Volunteers also are the ones to usually distribute the clothes and food. The only real cost to the Church is the cost of administration of these services and the storage space to keep the clothing and food supplies. But is this sacrificial love if it is virtually costless? When Jesus said He loved us He opened his arms wide and it cost Him his life. Are we really showing people the same sacrificial love of Jesus if our charity services do not cost us very much?

Housing, on the other hand, is very expensive to create and maintain. If a Church was to build an affordable apartment complex for the poor in their community it could cost them millions of dollars just to build, let alone maintain and keep running. Many of our Churches are building huge Church buildings that cost tens of millions of dollars to build and maintain yet they cannot build affordable housing for the poor. I can't help but wonder what Jesus would say to that situation? But there are some Churches that are providing affordable housing and I give them a standing ovation for their sacrifice!

There is a book that has recently been written by Jill Suzanne Shook that outlines the ministries of some of these Churches that have started to sacrificially give to develop affordable housing for the poor. That book is called "Making Housing Happen" and I highly recommend it if you and your Church want to start helping with housing. She describes one Church in Atlanta that turned an ex-prison into affordable housing and another Church in Chicago that turned an abandoned Hospital into affordable housing for the poor. The leaders of these Churches truly understood what it meant to be Shepherds to their people and they taught their people what it meant to sacrificially love one another.

Affordable housing is something I am very passionate about because without decent affordable housing people in poverty cannot move beyond their poverty. When a person is in need, the Church should be the first place they can go to for help. Yet, I have heard multiple stories about people in desperate need who knew that they could not turn to their Church to help meet that need. Overall, the Church has abdicated their responsibility to help the poor so the government has had to step in and take up the slack. Now this does not mean that all Churches do not help the poor. What this means is that the Church should be doing more to sacrificially give to the poor to show them the sacrificial love of Christ. The Scripture NEVER says that the Government should care for the poor. It says the Church should be caring for the poor.

***James 2:14-17** "What does it profit, my brethren, if someone says he has faith but does not have works? Can faith save him? 15 If a brother or sister is naked and destitute of daily food, 16 and one of you says to them, "Depart in peace, be warmed and filled," but you do not give them the things which are needed for the body, what does it profit? 17 Thus also faith by itself, if it does not have works, is dead."*

***Proverbs 14:21** "He who despises his neighbor sins; But he who has mercy on the poor, happy is he."*

***Proverbs 14:31** "He who oppresses the poor reproaches his Maker, But he who honors Him has mercy on the needy."*

Proverbs 19:17 "He who has pity on the poor lends to the Lord, And He will pay back what he has given."

There are also consequences for those that do not help the poor.

Proverbs 21:13 "Whoever shuts his ears to the cry of the poor will also cry himself and not be heard."

Most people need help at some time in their lives and thus this is a warning to those that refuse to hear the poor. When they refuse to listen, and help the poor and then some disaster hits their lives then their cries for help will also go unheard.

We have a tendency, here in the US, to condemn the poor and blame them for being poor. We judge and assume we understand the situation without truly finding out all the circumstances about a person's situation. This is completely wrong and God is not happy with this issue.

Instead of blaming the poor for being poor, maybe we should develop a relationship with them and find out what is really going on. A good shepherd gets to know the sheep to find out what their needs are and then does what needs to be done to meet those needs. Being a shepherd means that ALL the needs of the sheep are cared for, especially the basic needs of survival, which includes housing!

The second level is our safety or security needs. For people to grow and flourish they must feel safe and secure. The best illustration of safety needs are umbrellas. When we stand under an umbrella, we are submitting to that umbrella's protection. We also must hold the umbrella up if it is to do its job correctly. In the same way, when we submit to a Pastor, we are also submitting to his protection and for that protection to work, we must hold the Pastor up in prayer. But what happens if the umbrella does not do its job of protecting us from the rain?

Chapter 7: The Needs of the People

In this picture, I am standing under an umbrella frame. I am submitting to that umbrella and I am holding it up but because it is nothing but a frame that umbrella cannot protect me if I was to take it out in a rainstorm. In the same way, if a Pastor does not understand and accept his responsibility of protection then if we submit to that Pastor then we will get rained on and hurt even if we stay under their ministry and hold them up in prayer.

In this picture, I am standing under two umbrellas. You can see that one umbrella has holes in it but the top umbrella is perfect, with no holes. This represents Godly leadership. God is the perfect umbrella. His protection is perfect and will keep the rain off me. The second umbrella represents a Godly leader that understands and accepts and does his responsibility to the best of his ability. He will not do his job perfectly but if he stays under God's umbrella then the people under him will be protected.

Which umbrella would you choose to take out in a rainstorm? This is a perfect illustration of the leader's responsibility of protecting the people that stay in submission to him. If the shepherd is not protecting his flock as an umbrella protects then they are not doing their job and people will get hurt. And God will hold those leaders accountable for every person they allow to get rained on.

The third level of needs are our love and belonging needs. We need to have love in our life and feel like we belong somewhere. This level also includes our Spiritual needs which incorporates our need for God. God is love so if we must have love in our life to be successful then we must have God.

Chapter 7: The Needs of the People

Our Pastors preach "love your neighbor as you love yourself" but they do not teach how to do that. Preaching the "what" without teaching the "how" is useless. Love is an action, not an emotion! When Jesus died for us, He was showing us with His actions how much He loved us and He was also showing us how we are to love one another. We are to love one another with a sacrificial love. When we sacrificially love other people that means we put their needs ahead of our own needs.

Galatians 6:2 "Bear one another's burdens, and so fulfill the law of Christ."

Strong's Greek Dictionary defines the word "bear" as; "to take up in order to carry or bear; to put upon oneself (something) to be carried; to bear what is burdensome". I love the phrase "to put upon oneself". This is a very clear picture of what love means. We are to take upon ourselves other people's burdens so that they are easier to carry. We have lost the meaning of this concept today and even in the Church!

Galatians 6:2 says that when we bear one another's burdens we are fulfilling the Law of Christ. So, what is the Law of Christ? Jesus summed the Law up in these verses:

Matthew 22:37-40 "Jesus said to him, "'you shall love the Lord your God with all your heart, with all your soul, and with all your mind.' 38 This is the first and great commandment. 39 And the second is like it: 'You shall love your neighbor as yourself.' 40 On these two commandments hang all the Law and the Prophets."

When we 'bear one another's burdens', we are fulfilling the Law of Christ and that law is the Law of Love. This type of love is a sacrificial love that places the needs of others before the needs of ourselves. I see very little of this in today's Church.

The fourth level on this pyramid is our esteem needs. We must feel as if we are accomplishing something and are respected to be successful in life. These include self-esteem, confidence, achievement, recognition, and respect. As a Church, we should take pride in each person's accomplishments, even small accomplishments. We should encourage and lift each other up when we make mistakes. Without these needs being met people are not whole complete people.

1 Corinthians 12:26 "And if one member suffers, all the members suffer with it; or if one member is honored, all the members rejoice with it."

When we rejoice with those who rejoice and suffer with those who suffer then we are meeting people's esteem needs. By being there for one another through all of life's trials we show people that we truly love them and when we rejoice with them we are building them up.

The highest level is the need for self-actualization. This is the level at which we fulfill our potential and use the gifts God has given us to solve problems and help others. These needs include creativity, problem solving and morality. Every person deserves the chance to fulfill their God given potential. Leaders should be mentors and champions for their people and work with them to bring their gifts to their full potential. For a person to be truly successful in life all these needs must be met in some way.

I have said that the concept of Maslow's Hierarchy of needs is Biblical but the Hierarchy itself is not found in the Bible. The concept of Maslow's Hierarchy is to care for all the needs of the people, like a good shepherd cares for all the needs of his flock. Well, Jesus is the ultimate Good Shepherd so let's see if He satisfied all five levels of Maslow's Hierarchy of Needs.

Matthew 14:13-21 "When Jesus heard it, He departed from there by boat to a deserted place by Himself. But when the multitudes heard it, they followed Him on foot from the cities. 14 And when Jesus went out He saw a great multitude; and He was moved with compassion for them, and healed their sick. 15 When it was evening, His disciples came to Him, saying, "This is a deserted place, and the hour is already late. Send the multitudes away, that they may go into the villages and buy themselves food." 16 But Jesus said to them, "They do not need to go away. You give them something to eat." 17 And they said to Him, "We have here only five loaves and two fish." 18 He said, "Bring them here to Me." 19 Then He commanded the multitudes to sit down on the grass. And He took the five loaves and the two fish, and looking up to heaven, He blessed and broke and gave the loaves to the disciples; and the disciples gave to the multitudes. 2 So they all ate and were filled, and they took up twelve baskets full of the fragments that remained. 21 Now those who had eaten were about five thousand men, besides women and children."

Jesus cared for people's physical needs by feeding them. This is an example of Jesus fulfilling the first level of Maslow's Hierarchy of Needs. As I have stated before, many Churches do a halfway decent job at helping to care for the physical needs of the people.

Jesus also cared for the safety needs of his followers.

Chapter 7: The Needs of the People

Mark 4:35-41 "On the same day, when evening had come, He said to them, "Let us cross over to the other side." 36 Now when they had left the multitude, they took Him along in the boat as He was. And other little boats were also with Him. 37 And a great windstorm arose, and the waves beat into the boat, so that it was already filling. 38 But He was in the stern, asleep on a pillow. And they awoke Him and said to Him, "Teacher, do You not care that we are perishing?" 39 Then He arose and rebuked the wind, and said to the sea, "Peace, be still!" And the wind ceased and there was a great calm. 40 But He said to them, "Why are you so fearful? How is it that you have no faith?"41 And they feared exceedingly, and said to one another, "Who can this be, that even the wind and the sea obey Him!"

Jesus protected his disciples from a storm that would have killed them. Our Pastors may not be able to control the weather but they should be protecting their flock just as Jesus protected His disciples. If the shepherd is not protecting the flock, then he is not fulfilling his responsibility.

Jesus cared for the love and belonging needs of the people.

Luke 19:1-10 "Then Jesus entered and passed through Jericho. 2 Now behold, there was a man named Zacchaeus who was a chief tax collector, and he was rich. 3 And he sought to see who Jesus was, but could not because of the crowd, for he was of short stature. 4 So he ran ahead and climbed up into a sycamore tree to see Him, for He was going to pass that way. 5 And when Jesus came to the place, He looked up and saw him, and said to him, "Zacchaeus, make haste and come down, for today I must stay at your house." 6 So he made haste and came down, and received Him joyfully. 7 But when they saw it, they all complained, saying, "He has gone to be a guest with a man who is a sinner." 8 Then Zacchaeus stood and said to the Lord, "Look, Lord, I give half of my goods to the poor; and if I have taken anything from anyone by false accusation, I restore fourfold." 9 And Jesus said to him, "Today salvation has come to this house, because he also is a son of Abraham; 10 for the Son of Man has come to seek and to save that which was lost."

Zacchaeus was a tax collector and that made him an outcaste among his people. Yet Jesus showed him he was loved and accepted by choosing to go to his home to eat. Jesus was fulfilling Zacchaeus' love and belonging needs in this event. Just as Jesus did, Pastors need to embrace those who are outcaste and show them that they are loved and that they do belong somewhere.

Jesus also cared for the esteem needs of his disciples.

***Matthew 14:27-31** "But immediately Jesus spoke to them, saying, "Be of good cheer! It is I; do not be afraid." 28 And Peter answered Him and said, "Lord, if it is You, command me to come to You on the water." 29 So He said, "Come." And when Peter had come down out of the boat, he walked on the water to go to Jesus. 30 But when he saw that the wind was boisterous, he was afraid; and beginning to sink he cried out, saying, "Lord, save me!" 31 And immediately Jesus stretched out His hand and caught him, and said to him, "O you of little faith, why did you doubt?"*

Jesus allowed Peter to try and when he failed, Jesus was right there to pick him up. This helped to build Peter's self-esteem. Jesus fulfilled Peter's esteem needs in this story. Trying and failing is not failure. Never trying is the failure. Just as Jesus fulfilled Peter's esteem needs, Pastors need to encourage their people to step out and try new things, even if they fail on the first try.

And finally, Jesus cared for the self-actualization needs of his disciples.

***Acts 2:40-43** "And with many other words he (Peter) testified and exhorted them, saying, "Be saved from this perverse generation." 41 Then those who gladly received his word were baptized; and that day about three thousand souls were added to them. 42 And they continued steadfastly in the apostles' doctrine and fellowship, in the breaking of bread, and in prayers. 43 Then fear came upon every soul, and many wonders and signs were done through the apostles."*

This was the result of Peter's first sermon at Pentecost. Peter went from a man who always had his foot in his mouth to being the leader of the first Church! This happened because Jesus saw his potential and nurtured it thus fulfilling Peter's self-actualization needs. Just as Jesus nurtured Peter's self-actualization needs, Pastors must also nurture the self-actualization needs of their people.

With all of this, you may be thinking that I expect the Pastor to be perfect. Nothing could be further from the truth. Pastors and Church leaders do not have to be perfect. Peter was just a man and he was not perfect but he understood and accepted his responsibility of being a true shepherd for the people. Because of this, his ministry had a great Anointing and Power on it. Pastors and Church leaders are the umbrellas with holes in them. If they understand accept their Biblical job description and then try to fulfill that responsibility to the best of their ability, then God's Grace and Mercy will fill in the holes of their umbrellas and they would see a similar Anointing and Power on their ministry that Peter saw on his.

Pastors and Church leaders must remain humble. When they make a mistake, they should be willing to admit that mistake and do what they can to correct that mistake. Because the Pastors and Church leaders are not perfect, the people that follow them must be willing to forgive and give them another chance. Both sides in that relationship must do their part or the Church relationship will fail.

Amy Leigh Moore

Chapter 8

Practical Application

This job seems to be too big of a responsibility for the Pastor and will send them into even more burnout. We already have a big problem with Pastor burn-out so you may be thinking that this would just make a bad problem even worse.

Here are a few of the statistics on Pastor burnout. Per the New York Times (August 1, 2010) "Members of the clergy now suffer from obesity, hypertension and depression at rates higher than most Americans. In the last decade, their use of antidepressants has risen, while their life expectancy has fallen. Many would change jobs if they could."

- 13% of active pastors are divorced.

- 23% have been fired or pressured to resign at least once in their careers.

- 25% don't know where to turn when they have a family or personal conflict or issue.

- 25% of pastors' wives see their husband's work schedule as a source of conflict.

- 33% felt burned out within their first five years of ministry.

- 33% say that being in ministry is an outright hazard to their family.

- 40% of pastors and 47% of spouses are suffering from burnout, frantic schedules, and/or unrealistic expectations.

- 45% of pastors' wives say the greatest danger to them and their family is physical, emotional, mental, and spiritual burnout.

- 45% of pastors say that they've experienced depression or burnout to the extent that they needed to take a leave of absence from ministry.

- 50% feel unable to meet the needs of the job.
- 52% of pastors say they and their spouses believe that being in pastoral ministry is hazardous to their family's well-being and health.
- 56% of pastors' wives say that they have no close friends.
- 57% would leave the pastorate if they had somewhere else to go or some other vocation they could do.
- 70% don't have any close friends.
- 75% report severe stress causing anguish, worry, bewilderment, anger, depression, fear, and alienation.
- 80% of pastors say they have insufficient time with their spouse.
- 80% believe that pastoral ministry affects their families negatively.
- 90% feel unqualified or poorly prepared for ministry.
- 90% work more than 50 hours a week.
- 94% feel under pressure to have a perfect family.
- 1,500 pastors leave their ministries each month due to burnout, conflict, or moral failure.

How can Pastors accomplish the overwhelming responsibility of being a Biblical shepherd without working themselves to an early grave? That is why I have placed the job of the Pastor in the foundation of the Church. The Pastor is not to do the work of the ministry. They are to train the people to do the work of the ministry.

Ephesians 4:11-12 "And He Himself gave some to be apostles, some prophets, some evangelists, and some pastors and teachers, for the equipping of the saints for the work of ministry, for the edifying of the body of Christ"

The people have shirked their responsibility and they have put everything on the Pastor's shoulders and the Pastors and other leaders of the Church have allowed them to do this because they are afraid of offending the people. We have built the Church

Chapter 8: Practical Application

incorrectly so that not only is the reason that so many people are getting hurt in the Church, that is also the reason we have so much Pastor burnout.

> ***Matthew 16:15-19 "He said to them, "But who do you say that I am?" Simon Peter answered and said, "You are the Christ, the Son of the living God." Jesus answered and said to him, "Blessed are you, Simon Bar-Jonah, for flesh and blood has not revealed this to you, but My Father who is in heaven. And I also say to you that you are Peter, and on this rock I will build My church, and the gates of Hades shall not prevail against it. And I will give you the keys of the kingdom of heaven, and whatever you bind on earth will be bound in heaven, and whatever you loose on earth will be loosed in heaven."***

Jesus changed Simon's name to Peter and told Peter that he would be the "rock of the Church" in these verses. What exactly did He mean by that? There are two main interpretations of this event.

The Catholic Church has interpreted this passage to mean that Peter himself was the rock or foundation of the Church and that the Church was built on him and his spiritual descendants. This interpretation puts absolute power in the hands of those who claim to be the spiritual descendants of Peter, ie. The pope. But as history has shown, absolute power corrupts absolutely and thus the leadership of the Catholic Church has experienced massive corruption in its long history.

Protestants have argued that when Jesus said that Peter was the rock on which He would build His Church, He was meaning the revelation that Peter spoke. But this interpretation does not consider the reason Jesus changed Peter's name in the first place. Multitudes of people throughout history have received the same revelation from God but God has not changed the name of every person that received this revelation from Him. So, there must be a different reason that Jesus changed Peter's name and told him that "on this rock I will build my Church".

I believe that the reason Jesus changed Peter's name from Simon to Peter was because of the JOB that Jesus was giving him. As you read in a previous chapter, when Jesus reinstated Peter, He also was giving him the responsibility of being a true shepherd of the people. Peter understood this responsibility to mean that he was to care for ALL the needs of the people. We can see that he understood that by looking at Acts 4:34-35.

***Acts 4:34-35** "Nor was there anyone among them who lacked; for all who were possessors of lands or houses sold them, and brought the proceeds of the things that were sold, and laid them at the apostles' feet; and they distributed to each as anyone had need."*

Peter and the disciples understood that when Jesus told them to feed his sheep, He did not just mean to spiritually feed his sheep. Jesus meant that they should feed the sheep in all ways. When the Pastors understand that this is their responsibility, it can then become the rock or foundation on which the Church is built.

Now here is something that most people get tripped up by; the wealthy that sold their property and gave the proceeds to the disciples was not "what" they did but "how" they did it. What the disciples did was to accept their responsibility of being true shepherds of the people and taking care of ALL their needs. How they did that was by a supernatural anointing on the wealthy to love the less fortunate so much that they willingly gave up their property to make sure everyone had what they needed. This was not Socialism or Communism. This was a supernatural move of God's love on the people.

So, this brings up an interesting question. Why did God kill Ananias and his wife Sapphira?

***Acts 5:1-11** "But a certain man named Ananias, with Sapphira his wife, sold a possession. ²And he kept back part of the proceeds, his wife also being aware of it, and brought a certain part and laid it at the apostles' feet. ³But Peter said, "Ananias, why has Satan filled your heart to lie to the Holy Spirit and keep back part of the price of the land for yourself? ⁴While it remained, was it not your own? And after it was sold, was it not in your own control? Why have you conceived this thing in your heart? You have not lied to men but to God." ⁵Then Ananias, hearing these words, fell down and breathed his last. So great fear came upon all those who heard these things. ⁶And the young men arose and wrapped him up, carried him out, and buried him. ⁷Now it was about three hours later when his wife came in, not knowing what had happened. ⁸And Peter answered her, "Tell me whether you sold the land for so much?" She said, "Yes, for so much." ⁹ Then Peter said to her, "How is it that you have agreed together to test the Spirit of the Lord? Look, the feet of those who have buried your husband are at the door, and they will carry you out." ¹⁰Then immediately she fell down at his feet and breathed her last. And the young*

Chapter 8: Practical Application

men came in and found her dead, and carrying her out, buried her by her husband. [11]So great fear came upon all the church and upon all who heard these things."

The reason this couple was killed was because they tried to deceive God and the disciples for their own selfish reasons. But many people throughout history have lied to God and the Church for their own selfish reasons and God did not strike them dead. So, what else was going on here? Lying to God for their own selfish reasons was not only a sin but it also would have compromised the way in which the Church met the needs of the people thus undermining the shepherding of the Pastors. If this practice had been allowed, then the Power that was present in the Church would have also been compromised. This was a very serious threat and had to be dealt with seriously.

When our Pastor's accept that they are to be true shepherds of the people then God will provide another anointing to provide for "how" they are to fulfill those shepherding duties. But I doubt it will be the same way that the disciples did it. We live in a different time and a different culture so "how" this gets done will undoubtedly look different than it did in the book of Acts. But the "how" is not as important as the "what" at this moment. The "what" of a Pastor's responsibility is to be a true shepherd of the people and to care for ALL their needs, not just their spiritual needs. Once we understand the "what" then we can move on to the "how". Most Pastors have rejected the "what" because they don't know the "how". But they will never learn the "how" until they accept the "what".

Many people are visual learners so I have created a picture that shows what the full foundation of the Church should look like using Maslow's Hierarchy of Needs.

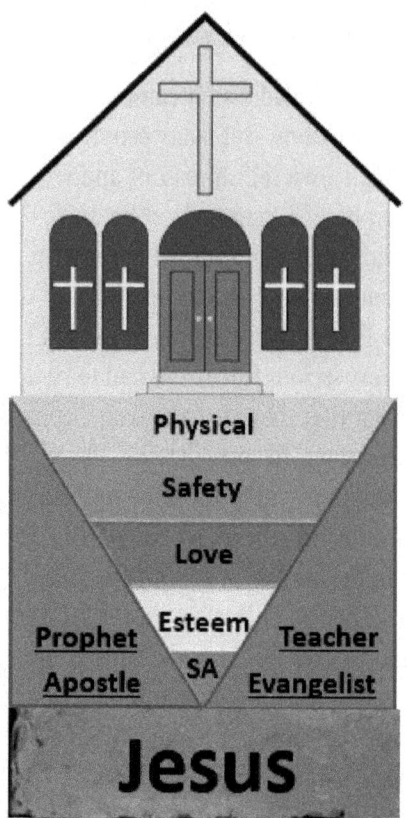

Maslow's Hierarchy represents the responsibility of the Pastor in this illustration. Notice that as we move closer to meeting the self-actualization needs of the people, we move closer to Jesus. Another aspect I want you to notice in this picture is that the Pastor supports the people to do the work of the ministry by meeting all their needs. The other four ministry gifts support the Pastor and Jesus supports them all as the Cornerstone. Yet, in many of our Churches we tell the people to support the Pastor and then expect the Pastor to do it all.

I have even talked with a Pastor that believed that the five-fold ministry gifts have ceased to exist and are now all vested in the Pastor. I was amazed that he could think this. We already have a major problem with Pastor burnout and he wanted to put even more on the Pastor's shoulders. I asked him to show me in Scripture where it explicitly says that God had discontinued the five-fold ministry gifts. Of course, he could not show me that Scripture because it does not exist.

Chapter 8: Practical Application

So, what would this look like in practice? The responsibility of being a shepherd is huge and much too big for the Pastor and his staff to do alone. Therefore, it is the foundation of the Church. ALL the programs, strategies, and systems the Church employs should be focused on meeting the needs of the people. The fivefold ministries gifts must work together to meet ALL the needs of the people. Every ministry of the Church should fulfill at least two levels of the needs from Maslow's Hierarchy. Let's examine the Small Group Ministry as an example.

Let's start with the physical needs of the people. These needs could be met very easily within the small group ministry if we start to teach the people to care for one another's needs. Many Pastor's will scoff and say that getting the people to take care of one another's needs is impossible. But I believe it is doable because the first Church did it in the book of Acts. So, let's look at what the first Church did and how it worked.

> *Acts 1:13-14 "And when they had entered, they went up into the upper room where they were staying: Peter, James, John, and Andrew; Philip and Thomas; Bartholomew and Matthew; James the son of Alphaeus and Simon the Zealot; and Judas the son of James. ¹⁴These all continued with one accord in prayer and supplication, with the women and Mary the mother of Jesus, and with His brothers."*
>
> *Acts 1:26 "And they cast their lots, and the lot fell on Matthias. And he was numbered with the eleven apostles."*
>
> *Matthew 13:55 "Is this not the carpenter's son? Is not His mother called Mary? And His brothers James, Joses, Simon, and Judas?"*
>
> *Acts 1:13-14 shows the senior leadership of the first church. These include the eleven disciples and Matthias (Acts 1:26), Mary, the Mother of Jesus, and His three brothers (Matthew 13:55). [James was a brother of Jesus but he was already numbered in the disciples]. This was a total of 16 people in Senior Leadership positions.*
>
> *Acts 1:15 "And in those days Peter stood up in the midst of the disciples (altogether the number of names was about a hundred and twenty)." There was a total of 120 people in the upper room when the Holy Spirit was given (Acts 1:15). To use today's language, we can assume that the other 104 people became leaders of smaller groups.*

Acts 2:41 "Then those who gladly received his word were baptized; and that day about three thousand souls were added to them."

Acts 2:44-47 "Now all who believed were together, and had all things in common, 45and sold their possessions and goods, and divided them among all, as anyone had need. 46So continuing daily with one accord in the temple, and breaking bread from house to house, they ate their food with gladness and simplicity of heart, 47 praising God and having favor with all the people. And the Lord added to the church daily those who were being saved."

Acts 4:34-35 "Nor was there anyone among them who lacked; for all who were possessors of lands or houses sold them, and brought the proceeds of the things that were sold, 35 and laid them at the apostles' feet; and they distributed to each as anyone had need."

Acts 5:14 "And believers were increasingly added to the Lord, multitudes of both men and women"

On the day of Pentecost about 3,000 people became Christians and joined that first church (Acts 2:41). Yet ALL the needs of the people in the Church were met (Acts 2:45 and 4:34-35) even as many more believers were added to their numbers (Acts 2:47 and 5:14).

I have believed for many years that these verses are the key to bringing the Church back to where it is supposed to be. When a lot of people read these verses, they see Socialism or Communism. But these verses have nothing to do with Socialism or Communism. Both Socialism and Communism are Government controlled systems in which the government forces the rich to give up their wealth to redistribute that wealth to the poor. These systems will NEVER work because the ruling class will ALWAYS have more than the people they rule. This is not true redistribution; if it was then the President or Government Leader would live in the exact same type of house as a janitor. But we can see that that has never happened and thus these systems will not work.

What the above verse in Acts does show us is true sacrificial Love in action. The people that sold their properties and gave the money to the Disciples to help the needy did not do so because they were forced to do so. They did this out of a true heart of

Love. But even this may not meet ALL the needs of the people. So how could they possibly meet ALL the needs of the people until "no one lacked anything"? Look again at this verse:

Acts 2:44-47 *"Now all who believed were together, and had all things in common, {sup}45{/sup}and sold their possessions and goods, and divided them among all, as anyone had need. {sup}46{/sup}So, continuing daily with one accord in the temple, and breaking bread from house to house, they ate their food with gladness and simplicity of heart, {sup}47{/sup} praising God and having favor with all the people. And the Lord added to the church daily those who were being saved."*

The Church in Acts did not just see each other once a week in a huge service. They ate together and lived together daily. They not only praised God once a week but regularly in different homes. This indicates that the needs must be met out of the small group ministry because that is the only ministry in the Church that meets in people's homes. This was vitally important in this Church!

So how do we bring the Church back to this? We have drifted so far away from these practices that if we tried to reintroduce this into the Church our Churches would dissolve from the rebellion of the people. Selling our property and donating ALL the money to the Church is too big for us now. So, we need to think smaller. How do we start to get people to take care of one another's needs?

This needs to be taught in the small groups. The Small Groups Ministry of a Church is where true relationship takes place and thus it should be the first place a person who has a need should be able to turn to. Every small group should have between 12 to 15 members and when a need arises among those small group members then the other members of the group should be the first ones to try to meet that need.

There is a procedure I have developed for this ministry. The small group can do any activity they want to if it involves interaction and developing of relationships. This could be a cooking group that gets together to try out new recipes or it could be a bunch of men that get together to play basketball. Most small groups will probably be a Bible study but it does not have to be limited to that. Whatever the activity, the last 30 minutes of the small group meeting should be set aside to discover people's needs and find ways to meet those needs.

During this last 30 minutes, the group leader will ask if anyone has any need that can be easily met during the next week. Small home or car repairs, gas money, or a ride to work, a free babysitter or help with housework or homework and hospital visitation are just a few examples of what I mean when I say small needs. When someone in the group expresses a need then that need is written down. Then the leader will ask for a volunteer to take care of that need. Each person in the group is only required to meet ONE need per week. When someone volunteers to meet that need then that person's name is also written down as the one to meet that need. If the need is bigger than one person can meet, then other members should volunteer to help meet the need. Then all the required information is given to the volunteers before the end of the meeting. Then the next week the leader will ask the person that expressed the need AND the volunteers to give a brief testimony about how meeting this need went. Was it a good experience; were there unforeseen problems, etc. This testimony time is a way for the leader to hold the group members accountable for caring for one another's needs.

The leader then writes a short weekly report about what needs were expressed, who volunteered to meet the need and if the need was met. This report is then sent to the Pastor that is over the small group ministry. Putting something like this in place will start to teach the people how to care for one another in the same way the Church in Acts cared for one another's needs. This will also take a huge amount of the pressure off the Pastor. If this is set up correctly, then all the Pastor must do is train the people, administer the program, and take care of any problems that arise. Putting a ministry like this in place could prevent a lot of Pastor burn-out while doing a much more effective job of meeting the people's needs then putting it all on the Pastor. It also will foster a lot more relationship then what we currently see in the Church!

So how do we meet the needs of the people that are not involved in the small group ministry? This is where a phone calling ministry comes into play. Every Sunday, the people should be encouraged to fill out Cards and put them into the offering plate. These cards will ask if they are members and if they are involved in a small group and if they are then what group they are involved in. Then a group of volunteers can go through the cards and anyone that is not involved in a small group is put on a calling list. The volunteers then divvy up the people on the calling list and they are called throughout the week.

When the phone volunteers call the people not involved in the small group ministry, they are not to ask, "Is there anything I can pray with you about?"

Instead they need to ask, "Is there any need that you have that we can meet?" The most important part of this ministry is the follow – through.

If one of the people on the phone says they have a need then the caller must make a note of it and then it is sent to a small group leader. This leader has the responsibility to meet that need, whether through the help of other people in the group or on his own. This need is also included in the small group leader's weekly report and in the weekly report made by the phone team. Both ministries should report to the same Pastor. Then the Pastor in charge of the small group ministry has the responsibility to make sure the need was met. This way even the needs of the people that may not be able to be involved in a small group can be met. If these types of ministries were put into place, then the benevolence ministry could be freed up to take care of the bigger needs in the Church and the needs of the community.

The Small Group Ministry could also provide for safety needs by providing a safe environment for people to truly be themselves and to deal with any pain they might be feeling. Each small group should be a safe place for people. It needs to be a place where people can be themselves without fear of judgment or condemnation. Life can be messy and the small group should be a place where people can start to make sense of the mess. To be able to do that they must feel safe enough to express themselves.

The Small Groups ministry is already the ministry in which relationships are built because it is the only ministry in which the people can get to know one another on a personal level so it meets the criteria for level three. The small group leader should try to make everyone feel as if they truly belong, even if that person is new to the group. No one should be shunned because they don't look like other people or they may be different in some way. Every person, no matter their color, size, or economic situation should be welcomed into the group.

Another way to meet the Love and Belonging Needs is to teach people how to love one another as they love themselves instead of just telling them to do it. Preaching the "what" without teaching the "how" is useless.

So how exactly do we 'love our neighbor as we love ourselves'? This is where faith comes into the picture. We are to "live by faith". If we are to "live by faith" then we must also "love by faith". Have you ever wondered what that phrase means? There are four different places in Scripture that say that "the just shall live by faith".

***Habakkuk 2:4** "Behold the proud, His soul is not upright in him; But the just shall live by his faith."*

***Galatians 3:11** "But that no one is justified by the law in the sight of God is evident, for "the just shall live by faith."*

Romans 1:17 *"For in it the righteousness of God is revealed from faith to faith; as it is written, "The just shall live by faith."*

Hebrews 10:38 *"Now the just shall live by faith; But if anyone draws back, My soul has no pleasure in him."*

Just by looking at the Scripture references we can see that living by faith is three times more important for those of us that live under the New Covenant then it was for those living under the Old Covenant. We can see this because only one of the four Scripture references is in the Old Testament and three of them are in the New Testament.

So, what does it mean to actually live by faith? To answer this question, I want to take a close look at one of my favorite Bible stories; "The Woman with the Issue of Blood".

Mark 5:25-34 *"Now a certain woman had a flow of blood for twelve years, 26 and had suffered many things from many physicians. She had spent all that she had and was no better, but rather grew worse. 27When she heard about Jesus, she came behind Him in the crowd and touched His garment. 28For she said, "If only I may touch His clothes, I shall be made well." 29Immediately the fountain of her blood was dried up, and she felt in her body that she was healed of the affliction. 30And Jesus, immediately knowing in Himself that power had gone out of Him, turned around in the crowd and said, "Who touched My clothes?" 31But His disciples said to Him, "You see the multitude thronging You, and You say, 'Who touched Me?'" 32And He looked around to see her who had done this thing. 33But the woman, fearing and trembling, knowing what had happened to her, came and fell down before Him and told Him the whole truth. 34And He said to her, "Daughter, your faith has made you well. Go in peace, and be healed of your affliction."*

This woman must have been in a great deal of pain and emotional distress after 12 years of suffering with this problem. But she did not let that stop her from going after Jesus. She heard about Jesus; that He was a healer and had compassion on the sick and she made a conscious decision to pursue Him. Then she acted on that decision. She not only said she would touch His clothes but she did it!

Our faith is the same as hers. Our faith must have action if it will bring any results. In fact, I would go as far to say that our actions are our faith. So, to make this very simple; faith is a conscious decision to believe what God says is true and then to act on that decision. If we are to live by faith and faith is a conscious decision to believe that what God says in His Word is true and then to act on that decision and love is part of life, then we can also love by faith!

So how exactly do we love by faith? Well to answer this question let's look at what Jesus said about love.

Matthew 22:37-39 "You shall love the LORD your God with all your heart, with all your soul, and with all your mind. This is the first and great commandment. And the second is like it: you shall love your neighbor as yourself."

How many steps are seen in the above verses? Most people would say two but there are four. A person cannot love God until she firmly believes that He loves her.

I John 4:19 "We love Him because He first loved us."

People also cannot love their neighbors unless they fully love themselves. So, these steps are:

1. Make a conscious decision to believe that God loves you and then act on it.
2. Make a conscious decision to love Him in the same way that He loves you and then act on it.
3. Make a conscious decision to love yourself as God loves you and then act on it.
4. Make a conscious decision to love your neighbor as you love yourself and then act on it.

Something that was an amazing revelation to me was that people do not love others because they do not love themselves. I never truly suffered from this problem. I guess it was because I was born again at the age of four that I, for the most part, thought that I had value and I had a good feeling of self-worth most of the time. Consequently, it never dawned on me that most people don't love themselves so there is no way they can truly love others. This problem is rampant in our churches. One would think that in the church, especially, there would be love, but I have found out through painful experience that there is very little love in our churches because Christians don't truly believe that God loves them just as they are and they don't truly love themselves. Without those two beliefs, it is no wonder they can't love others. This can be taught in the small groups very effectively. At the end of this book, I have included a 15-week small group Bible study to teach people how to love God, themselves, and other people.

To meet the esteem needs of the people means that the small group participates should build up one another and celebrate even small successes and bear one another's burdens to build up a person's self - esteem. The people in the group should care enough about one another to "mourn with those who mourn and rejoice with those who rejoice".

Romans 12:15 "Rejoice with those who rejoice, and weep with those who weep."

Failures should not be condemned but the person that failed should be encouraged to try again and not give up. Not succeeding is not a failure, never trying is the failure. So, people should be encouraged to try new things and supported when they do not succeed.

The last level can be met in the Small Groups ministry by providing training and an environment for people to fulfill their potential. Train up members to be leaders and don't allow prejudice to get in the way. All the people should be encouraged to stretch themselves and do something they have never done before to fulfill their God-given potential. Also, leadership training should not be something they must pay for. If they need to buy a book that is fine but otherwise leadership training should be free to those who want to be small group leaders.

When designed correctly, the Small Groups ministry can fulfill every level on this pyramid. Every other ministry in the Church should strive to be able to do the same thing but if they can't then at a minimum they should be able to fulfill at least two levels on Maslow's pyramid. Senior Pastors should encourage their Ministry Leaders to think creatively and get outside the box on how to meet these needs.

By setting up the Church in this way, the responsibility of the shepherd becomes part of the foundation of the Church and everyone is working toward the goal of meeting all the needs of the people. This would mean that more of the needs are being met and less people are being hurt and forgotten about and this also takes the pressure off the Senior Pastor, thus decreasing Pastor burnout. This is a win/win for everyone in the Church.

Chapter 9

The Benevolence Ministry

By teaching the people to care for one another's smaller needs in the small group ministry we can free up the benevolence ministry to take care of the bigger needs of the people such as housing and it also frees up the benevolence ministry to care for the needs of the community.

Meeting the needs of the people will take money so the first change I will propose is a change in the way the money is distributed in the Church. When a Pastor preaches on money, one of the first verses that they use is Malachi 3:8-10

"Will a man rob God? Yet you have robbed Me! But you say, 'In what way have we robbed You?' In tithes and offerings. ⁹You are cursed with a curse, for you have robbed Me, Even this whole nation. ¹⁰Bring all the tithes into the storehouse, That there may be food in My house, And try Me now in this," Says the Lord of hosts, "If I will not open for you the windows of heaven And pour out for you such blessing That there will not be room enough to receive it."

Many Pastors use this Scripture to try to convince the people to bring 10% of their income into the Church so that there can be Spiritual food in the Church for the people. This Spiritual food is supposedly the sermons that the Pastor preaches every Sunday morning. Well, I want to dig into this Scripture a bit further and I will end up turning this interpretation on its ear.

Who is God talking to in these verses? Most Pastors will say that He is talking to the people but that is not substantiated by the Scripture itself. Malachi 1:6 gives us the first indication of who God was talking to in Malachi.

Malachi 1:6 "A son honors his father, and a servant his master. If then I am the Father, Where is My honor? And if I am a Master, Where is My reverence? Says the

Lord of hosts to you priests who despise My name. Yet you say, 'In what way have we despised Your name?'

So, Malachi 1 says that God is talking to the priests or the leaders of the Church at that time. Well, maybe it was just for that one verse? So, let's see if we can find another place in Malachi that states who God is talking to.

Malachi 2:1 "And now, O priests, this commandment is for you."

Malachi 2:4a "Then you shall know that I have sent this commandment to you, That My covenant with Levi may continue,"

Well this is interesting. In both chapters 1 and 2 God says He is talking to the priests and the Levites, who were the Priestly tribe of the Israelites. So, in these two chapters God is talking to the leadership of the Church and, suddenly, He changes his audience in chapter 3 to talk to the people? I do not see any evidence of that. God is talking to the priests throughout this whole book and thus Chapter 3 is also meant for the leadership of the Church.

When God asks if a man will rob God in Malachi 3:8, he is not just talking to any man but to the leadership of the Church specifically. He is commanding the Church leaders to tithe off the income that comes into the Church. I don't know how many Churches tithe because Churches do not have to report their finances to the IRS.

So, if a Church should tithe, then where does that tithe go? Well, to answer that, let's look back at Malachi 3:10.

"Bring all the tithes into the storehouse, that there may be food in My house, And try Me now in this," Says the Lord of hosts, "If I will not open for you the windows of heaven And pour out for you such blessing That there will not be room enough to receive it."

What if God literally means physical food should be available in His house and not just Spiritual food? If the food God is talking about is literally physical food and not Spiritual food, then maybe the place the Church should be tithing is into the benevolence ministry so that there will literally be food in His house for the people. Wow! What a radical thought! The Church should be tithing back to the people! Wouldn't that be a major first step toward truly meeting ALL the needs of the people just like a shepherd meets ALL the needs of the sheep?

Chapter 9: The Benevolence Ministry

Most Churches that do tithe, tithe to other ministries because they interpret that word 'food' as spiritual food. However, the Hebrew word for 'food' in this text means prey, food, or leaf. We prey on animals for physical food and we eat leaves or plants for physical food. I see no indication that the Hebrew word is meaning Spiritual food. I believe this has been a misinterpretation of the word 'food' by someone long ago and the interpretation that this meant Spiritual food has been passed down through generation after generation because no one has studied it out to find out its true meaning.

So, this idea boils down to this; the Church invests 10% of their total income back into their benevolence ministry to meet the physical needs of the people. The benevolence ministry has become the most pulled upon ministry in recent years because of the economic downturn but it is usually the least funded ministry of the Church. Again, this cannot be substantiated because the Church does not have to report their finances to the IRS but I think most churches only fund their benevolence programs with 1% or 2% of their total income. I believe that some Churches may go as high as 5% but I cannot be sure about that. Imagine the help the Church could give people if they funded their benevolence ministries with a full 10% of their income.

Per Charity Navigator, which is one of the best sites for tracking nonprofit organizations, total giving was more than $390 billion to nonprofits in the US in 2016. 32% of all donations ($122.94 billion) went to Religious organizations. If the Church would tithe off that into their benevolence ministry, then we could greatly decrease the size of the Government Welfare programs. The amount that would be available to help the poor through Church Benevolence programs if the Church tithed to those programs would be approximately $12.3 Billion. Imagine what could be done to help the poor with that kind of money.

If we are to fund the benevolence ministry with a full 10% of the Church's income, how can we safeguard it against people that will try to defraud the Church? This is a legitimate question and I am fully aware that there are people out there that will take advantage of the generosity of the Church. Therefore, we must be even more diligent and look beyond the surface of the people that need our help.

Take some of the extra money that is being put into the benevolence ministry and create a data base in which every person that asks for help from the benevolence ministry has their and their family's names and pictures in a computer file as well as all their relevant personal information and what help they needed. This data base is then shared with every Church and charity organization in the city or county. Each time a person goes to a ministry in that area their file is upgraded.

How can this help the Church to help the people? Well, many people who are trying to scam the system jump from one Church to another looking for handouts. This system will show who is running these types of scams and the Church can work together to help eliminate this problem.

So, how do we eliminate these scammers from the system? When a worker in the benevolence program enters the information of the person asking for help, the database will show the history of that person's need. If Sally goes into Church A's benevolence ministry for help on June first and then on June 15th she shows up at Church B's benevolence ministry asking for the same type of help, this database will show this. If the worker sees a pattern developing they can ask more questions to find out why the person is going from Church to Church looking for help. The other thing a worker can do is to ask for someone else to verify their story. A friend or someone they knew from their job or school could verify a person's story. If the person has been injured or sick, then they should have medical documentation to back that up. Then the worker can find a way to help the underlying problem instead of just giving them a handout. A person that is scamming is not going to want a worker to look closer at the reasons they are asking for help and they most definitely do not want a benevolence worker trying to verify their story.

I was watching an episode of "Touched by an Angel" many years ago, and something stuck out at me. In this episode, Monica became homeless so she could help someone who was homeless. The man she was sent to help had a bad knee and thus could no longer do menial labor jobs. He was on the side of the street holding a sign asking for help when another man in a Cadillac pulled up beside him.

The man in the Cadillac rolled down his window and said to the homeless man, "I have a job laying carpet if you are interested?"

The homeless man knew he could not do that job because of his bad knee so he had to turn the job down. The man in the Cadillac shook his head and as he drove away we could hear him say, "No good lazy bum!"

The homeless man was not lazy. He was injured so he could no longer do menial labor jobs. If someone comes into the benevolence minister's office and the minister pulls up the database and finds this same man has gone from Church to Church looking for help yet he has not found a job and looks perfectly healthy, then the minister should dig a bit deeper and find out what is the real problem. If the man was the homeless man from the above example, he may say, "I am trained as a carpet layer but because I hurt my knee I can no longer do that type of work." If he was truly injured, then he should have medical documentation to verify this.

Well, instead of dismissing this homeless man, maybe the minister can help him get trained for a desk job and give him the emotional and financial help he needs until he gets retrained and finds a job he can do. This is the purpose behind this database idea.

In my experience, most people are not willing to go beyond the surface and see what the real reason may be for someone needing help. This database is a way to help the benevolence minister and workers to see beyond the surface and to help with the root cause of the problem. Sometimes a handout is not what someone needs but instead a hand up is what they need and this database can be the first step in identifying someone that just needs a hand up verses someone who is just looking for a handout.

To put this idea into practice means that the Churches and Charity Ministries in an area must work together and cooperate. If the Churches will put aside their doctrinal disagreements and truly try to help the people of the community like the shepherds the Bible says they are to be then this could bring some unity back into the Church.

I read a book in one of my nonprofit classes about Faith Based Management in Churches and this man said that it was a fact that Churches compete with one another. That may be a fact but this competition is not what God intended.

1 Corinthians 12:12-27 "For as the body is one and has many members, but all the members of that one body, being many, are one body, so also is Christ. 13For by one Spirit we were all baptized into one body—whether Jews or Greeks, whether slaves or free—and have all been made to drink into one Spirit. 14For in fact the body is not one member but many. 15If the foot should say, "Because I am not a hand, I am not of the body," is it therefore not of the body? 16And if the ear should say, "Because I am not an eye, I am not of the body," is it therefore not of the body? 17If the whole body were an eye, where would be the hearing? If the whole were hearing, where would be the smelling? 18But now God has set the members, each one of them, in the body just as He pleased. 19And if they were all one member, where would the body be? 20But now indeed there are many members, yet one body. 21And the eye cannot say to the hand, "I have no need of you"; nor again the head to the feet, "I have no need of you." 22No, much rather, those members of the body which seem to be weaker are necessary. 23And those members of the body which we think to be less honorable, on these we bestow greater honor; and our unpresentable parts have greater modesty,

[24] but our presentable parts have no need. But God composed the body, having given greater honor to that part which lacks it, [25] that there should be no schism in the body, but that the members should have the same care for one another. [26] And if one member suffers, all the members suffer with it; or if one member is honored, all the members rejoice with it. [27] Now you are the body of Christ, and members individually.

If we are ALL a body, then we need to be cooperating as the body cooperates. The eye does not compete with the ear in our physical bodies. They work together in harmony so that we can function to the best of our ability. This means that different Churches have no business competing with one another. We should be working together not competing against one another.

When I was in a class called "Church Administration" for my Theology degree, one thing that was said in that class has stood out in my mind. Another student raised his hand and told a short story. "I was in a small group in another's person's home and we were talking about whether the Church is a business or a body. When a thirteen-year-old child said something that caused all of us to sit in stunned silence. The child said, 'When a body becomes a business, isn't that called prostitution?' We were stunned and God's conviction fell on us and we fell on our faces in tears."

That child's statement is very true and many of our Churches have become businesses and that is why they compete with one another. Businesses compete for available dollars but the Church is not a business. Yes, there are some business aspects to the Church and good financial practices must be used but the Church is not a business. The Church is the Body of Christ yet we have been acting like the Business of Christ. Essentially, this is prostitution.

This database idea will only work if ALL the Churches work together. If we compete against one another and fight over doctrinal differences, then Satan has already defeated us and the people's needs are not getting met and more people are getting hurt.

Chapter 10

Evaluation

By designing a Church using Maslow's Hierarchy of Needs, we are giving ourselves a new way to evaluate Church performance. We are also holding the leaders accountable for being good shepherds. With these new evaluation tools, we can see where the weaknesses in the Church are and try to strengthen those weaknesses.

Currently, most Churches use attendance of the Sunday morning service and the amount of money that came in the offering as their evaluation tools. But how does this help the Church leaders become better shepherds of the people? Using these evaluation tools do not truly help the Church become better. These things are easy to keep track of but they do not show us if the people are getting truly discipled nor if their needs are being met. Most Pastors and Church leaders do not understand their full responsibility and they think the goal of the Church is to reach as many people as possible. They have reduced the Great Commission down to making converts instead of making disciples. When this happens, Church does become a numbers game so it makes sense to use numbers as the measure of success.

But the Pastor's responsibility is not to make converts but to make disciples and the best way to make disciples is through relationship and meeting ALL the needs of the people in the same way a shepherd meets ALL the needs of the sheep. Since this job is different than what most Pastors think it is then the measures of success must be different than they originally thought they were as well.

The following chart could be used to evaluate whether all the needs of the people are being met. The Senior Pastor and his staff should be able to keep track of what levels of Maslow's each ministry is fulfilling and they can see if any level is not being taken care of as well as other levels. This could be done very easily with a simple chart.

	Benevolence	Small Groups	Children's	Youth	Outreach
Physical	X	X			
Safety	X	X	X	X	
Love & Belonging		X	X	X	X
Esteem		X	X	X	X
Self-Actualization		X			

By looking at the above chart, the Senior Pastor and his staff can see that the Love and Belonging Needs, Safety Needs and Esteem Needs are being met very well. The Physical Needs and Self-Actualization Needs could be improved upon. They could then get together with some of the Ministry Leaders to brainstorm how to meet the Physical Needs and Self-Actualization Needs more effectively.

Another evaluation tool that we could use would be a needs ratio. We can compare how many needs were expressed to how many needs were met. Imagine that 400 needs were expressed but only 200 of those needs were met. Then the needs ratio would be 400/200. When divided out this is 2. Now imagine that 400 needs were expressed in the Church but this time 300 of those needs were met. When expressed in a ratio that would be 400/300 or 1.3333. So, the closer the needs ratio is to 1, the better the Church is at meeting the needs of the people.

This can be done in the small groups ministry if we teach the people how to care for one another's needs as I illustrated earlier. It can also be done in the benevolence ministry and any other ministry that has physical needs as one of the levels of Maslow's that they are fulfilling. This would align itself much better with the true responsibility of the Pastor than using attendance and offering numbers.

Another evaluation tool we could employ are congregation surveys. Church leaders could design and distribute surveys to the congregation to evaluate the leadership on their effectiveness of meeting all 5 levels of Maslow's. This will show us if the leaders need some improvement in being good shepherds. Here is an example of a congregation survey that could be developed.

Chapter 10: Evaluation

How effectively does your Church meet the physical needs of the people?

    __very effectively

    __somewhat effectively

    __neutral

    __somewhat ineffectively

    __very ineffectively

How effectively does your Church meet the safety needs of the people?

    __very effectively

    __somewhat effectively

    __neutral

    __somewhat ineffectively

    __very ineffectively

How effectively does your Church meet the love and belonging needs of the people?

    __very effectively

    __somewhat effectively

    __neutral

    __somewhat ineffectively

    __very ineffectively

How effectively does your Church meet the esteem needs of the people?

    __very effectively

    __somewhat effectively

    __neutral

    __somewhat ineffectively

    __very ineffectively

How effectively does your Church meet the self-actualization needs of the people?

    __very effectively

    __somewhat effectively

    __neutral

    __somewhat ineffectively

    __very ineffectively

These questions are just a general example of this evaluation tool. These questions can be broken down to more specific questions aimed at each individual Church. This could be a very effective tool in evaluating whether the leadership are being true shepherds in the eyes of the congregation. Other questions that could be asked are how the leadership could improve their shepherding skills. There are many things that could be done with this survey to help improve the shepherding skills of the leadership. One other question that could be asked on this survey is how could that person, as part of the congregation help to meet the needs of the other people in the congregation.

By using these evaluation tools, we can see how the Church is doing in meeting the needs of the people and if there are deficiencies, the leadership can start to experiment to improve on those deficiencies. Evaluation is an ongoing process and it is a vital part of the process. Without evaluation, leaders cannot know whether they are doing the right job in the right way.

Chapter 11

Warnings and Rewards for Shepherds

When Jesus reinstated Peter He was also handing the Shepherding baton off to Peter and subsequently every Pastor that came after Peter. But what happens when the Pastors do not know their responsibility and thus fail to do their job? Well, God promises that He will not leave us without a shepherd. He will send someone else who will truly shepherd His flock.

Jeremiah 23:1-4 "Woe to the shepherds who destroy and scatter the sheep of My pasture!" says the Lord. ² Therefore thus says the Lord God of Israel against the shepherds who feed My people: "You have scattered My flock, driven them away, and not attended to them. Behold, I will attend to you for the evil of your doings," says the Lord. ³ "But I will gather the remnant of My flock out of all countries where I have driven them, and bring them back to their folds; and they shall be fruitful and increase. ⁴ I will set up shepherds over them who will feed them; and they shall fear no more, nor be dismayed, nor shall they be lacking," says the Lord."

God's priority is to the people and He is deeply grieved that the shepherds who He placed over the flock have not been doing the job He commanded them to do. Because they are not fulfilling their responsibility, He promises to raise up new shepherds who will fulfill the responsibility He wants them to. Here is another Scripture that gives a warning to shepherds who are not truly doing the shepherding job they are supposed to be doing.

Ezekiel 34: 1-10 "The word of the Lord came to me: "Son of man, prophesy against the shepherds of Israel; prophesy, and say to them, even to the shepherds, Thus, says the Lord God: Ah, shepherds of Israel who have been feeding yourselves! Should not shepherds feed the sheep? You eat the fat, you clothe yourselves with the wool, you slaughter the fat ones, but you do not feed the sheep. The weak you have not strengthened, the sick you have not healed, the injured you have not bound up, the strayed you have not brought back, the lost you have not sought, and with force and harshness you have ruled them. So, they were scattered, because there was no shepherd, and they became food for all the wild beasts. Therefore, O shepherds, hear the word of the Lord! Thus, says the Lord God: "Behold, I am against the shepherds, and I will require My flock at their hand; I will cause them to cease feeding the sheep, and the shepherds shall feed themselves no more; for I will deliver My flock from their mouths, that they may no longer be food for them."

There is also a Scripture in the New Testament that warns Pastors to be careful about how they shepherd the flock.

Acts 20:28 *"Therefore take heed to yourselves and to all the flock, among which the Holy Spirit has made you overseers, to shepherd the church of God which He purchased with His own blood."*

God does not want His people hurt and He is grieved over all of this. He hurts when His people hurt. He will not allow His people to be hurt for long.

But not everything is doom and gloom and bad news. For those Pastors that are being a true shepherd there is some wonderful news. God is pleased with those Pastors that are truly shepherds for their people and He promises great rewards for those that are fulfilling the responsibility He called them to do.

1 Timothy 3:13 *"For those who have served well as deacons obtain for themselves a good standing and great boldness in the faith which is in Christ Jesus."*

In today's world, we need people with "great boldness and good standing" to bring Truth to a dying world. Every preacher I know of would love to have this type of boldness in proclaiming the Gospel but few of them are willing to be the shepherds they are supposed to be to obtain this boldness.

1 Timothy 5:17 *"Let the elders who rule well be counted worthy of double honor, especially those who labor in the word and doctrine."*

Notice this verse says, "the elders who **rule well**". This promise is not just for any elder but those elders that rule well as a shepherd rules. I know there must be some out there and God promises that those shepherds will receive double honor. What an amazing promise!

1 Peter 5:1-4 "The elders who are among you I exhort, I who am a fellow elder and a witness of the sufferings of Christ, and also a partaker of the glory that will be revealed: ² Shepherd the flock of God which is among you, serving as overseers, not by compulsion but willingly, not for dishonest gain but eagerly; ³ nor as being lords over those entrusted to you, but being examples to the flock; ⁴ and when the Chief Shepherd appears, you will receive the crown of glory that does not fade away."

That crown of glory is what every true Christian desire more than anything else; to be able to finish our race and hear Jesus say, "Well done, my good and faithful servant." I know that is my greatest desire and in this Scripture God is promising a Pastor who is a good shepherd, caring for the needs of his people above his own needs; a crown that will NEVER fade! This is one of the most amazing promises in the Bible but there is a condition attached to it. Not every shepherd will receive this crown. Only the Shepherds who cares for the flock with love and not for personal gain will receive this crown!

This is a very serious issue in God's eyes and He has promised huge rewards for those that shepherd His people properly. He also gave dire warnings for those Pastors that do not shepherd His people as they should. I pray that more Pastors come out on the reward side then on the warning side.

I also want to reiterate that a good shepherd does not have to be a perfect shepherd. We all make mistakes but a good shepherd will be humble enough to admit those mistakes and do whatever he can to fix those mistakes. Earthly leaders are the umbrellas with holes in it but if those holey leaders will remain humble and stay submitted to God's umbrella then God will fill in the holes. This type of leader will be the one that receives the rewards from God!

Amy Leigh Moore

Chapter 12

Expected Results

When we build the Church on a complete Foundation then we can accomplish the same things the Disciples did.

Acts 2:43-47 "Then fear came upon every soul, and many wonders and signs were done through the apostles. 44 Now all who believed were together, and had all things in common, 45 and sold their possessions and goods, and divided them among all, as anyone had need. 46 So continuing daily with one accord in the temple, and breaking bread from house to house, they ate their food with gladness and simplicity of heart, 47 praising God and having favor with all the people. And the Lord added to the church daily those who were being saved."

Acts 4:34-35 "Nor was there anyone among them who lacked; for all who were possessors of lands or houses sold them, and brought the proceeds of the things that were sold, 35 and laid them at the apostles' feet; and they distributed to each as anyone had need."

We may not accomplish this in the same way that they did but we can still accomplish it. I also believe that when we build the Church on a complete foundation, we can expect that God will pour out the same type of Anointing and Power that the Church in Acts saw. And when God pours out that type of Anointing, it will fill in the holes of the leadership. Peter and the disciples were imperfect men and they made mistakes but the Anointing that God poured out on their ministry covered those mistakes. Church leaders can have that same type of Anointing and Covering if they would do what the disciples did.

Acts 5:12-16 "And through the hands of the apostles many signs and wonders were done among the people. And they were all with one accord in Solomon's Porch. Yet none of the rest dared join them, but the people esteemed them highly. And believers were increasingly added to the Lord, multitudes of both men and women, so that they brought the sick out into the streets and laid them on beds and couches, that at least the shadow of Peter passing by might fall on some of them. Also, a multitude gathered from the surrounding cities to Jerusalem, bringing sick people and those who were tormented by unclean spirits, and they were all healed."

Building a Church on a complete foundation will fulfill Hebrews 13:17.

Hebrews 13:17 *"Obey those who rule over you, and be submissive, for they watch out for your souls, as those who must give account. Let them do so with joy and not with grief, for that would be unprofitable for you."*

The leaders will truly be watching out for the souls of their people. When the people see that the leaders are truly doing their job then they will submit joyfully. I know I would. I would love to see a Church leader design his Church this way. If I could find this type of Church I would be the first person to sign up as a member.

Building the Church on a complete foundation will minimize Church Hurt. We may not be able to eliminate Church hurt but we can minimize it if we build the Church on a complete foundation. This will also effectively close the back door of the Church. Many times, people have left because they have gotten hurt and instead of confronting the issue they leave quietly and suffer in silence.

When we construct the Church on a complete foundation then ALL the Great Commission will be the natural result!

Matthew 28:19-20 *"Go therefore and make disciples of all the nations, baptizing them in the name of the Father and of the Son and of the Holy Spirit, teaching them to observe all things that I have commanded you; and lo, I am with you always, even to the end of the age." Amen."*

When we construct the Church on a complete foundation, we are not only converting people but we would also be making disciples like Jesus commanded us to do through love and relationships and meeting each other's needs.

Chapter 13

To Those Who Have Been Hurt in the Church

This book has been about how to prevent Church hurt from happening but there are millions of people out there who have already suffered from Church hurt and this chapter is for you. We need to work on both sides of the equation. We need to prevent Church hurt from happening but we also need to help heal those who have already been hurt in the Church.

So, you may ask why does God allow people to get hurt in the first place? God gave us free will and He willingly limited His own power so we could have that free will. God does not cause bad things to happen but if we allow Him, He can turn what was meant for bad and work it out for our good. I believe that bad things happen because of four reasons. Bad things can happen because of one of these reasons or a combination of these reasons.

1. We make bad decisions that affect our lives. A person that has smoked for all his life should not be surprised when he is diagnosed with lung cancer.

2. Other people make bad decisions that affect us. A drunk man decides to get behind the wheel and a wife and mother are killed when he runs a red light.

3. Because of sin, God placed a curse on this earth. Genesis 3:17 *"Then to Adam He said, "Because you have heeded the voice of your wife, and have eaten from the tree of which I commanded you, saying, 'You shall not eat of it': "Cursed is the ground for your sake; In toil, you shall eat of it All the days of your life."*

4. Satan is real and he is out to destroy us. John 10:10 *"**The thief does not come except to steal, and to kill, and to destroy. I have come that they may have life, and that they may have it more abundantly."***

For those of you that have been hurt by the Church, please remember that God was not the source of that pain. If you believe that God caused your pain, then you will turn away from the One Person that can heal that pain.

I understand your pain and your anger. I was deeply hurt, by many different Churches, and I was angry about it for a long time. Anger is a natural and very human response to an injustice. There is nothing wrong with being angry or feeling the pain when someone has hurt you. But you cannot let that hurt and anger consume you and take over your life. If you want to get past the anger and the pain you must forgive and let God heal you.

I have heard many Pastors preach on forgiveness and some of them say that forgiveness is a process. I disagree. Forgiveness is an instantaneous conscious decision we make that starts the process of healing. Reread that last sentence. Yes, I said forgiveness is a choice and healing is a process. I feel very strongly about this and I believe that most people have confused the two. Here is why I believe forgiveness can never be a process.

Mark 11:25-26 ""And whenever you stand praying, if you have anything against anyone, forgive him, that your Father in heaven may also forgive you your trespasses. 26 But if you do not forgive, neither will your Father in heaven forgive your trespasses."

This verse tells us to forgive someone as "we stand praying". A process takes time and if forgiveness was a process then God would be unjust in commanding us to forgive as "we stand praying". A process cannot be done instantaneously yet God tells us we can forgive while we pray. This means that forgiveness must be a conscious choice that we make. You do not have to "feel" like forgiving someone to forgive them. This is what making a conscious decision is all about. We can decide to do something whether we feel like it or not.

How many of you "feel" like going to work every day? You go to work because you know you must and because you have a family to support and you have bills to pay. You make a conscious decision to go to work even when you don't "feel" like it. The

Chapter 13: To Those Who Have Been Hurt in the Church

same way you make that decision is how you make the decision to forgive. Not because you "feel" like it but because you know you must, to be healed.

Another reason I believe that forgiveness is an instantaneous conscious decision is that understanding forgiveness in this way prevents Satan from putting condemnation on those who have been hurt.

Romans 8:1 "There is therefore now no condemnation to those who are in Christ Jesus, who do not walk according to the flesh, but according to the Spirit."

If we believe that forgiveness is a process, then when we feel the pain, Satan can whisper condemnation in our ears. He can say, "See, you still feel the pain so you must not have forgiven." But if we understand that forgiveness is a conscious decision we make then we can tell Satan to get lost and say, "I have forgiven but I am not through the healing process yet. So, Satan, you can take a hike."

Forgiveness is not about the other person. It is about you and your healing. God showed me what forgiveness was 20 years ago, by showing me a picture of someone with a broken arm and asking me, "What does the doctor do to fix a broken arm?"

I answered, "He puts a caste on it."

Then God asked me, "What does the caste do to heal the broken arm?"

I replied, "It holds the arm in place so the body can heal itself."

I then heard God say, "Exactly and that is also what forgiveness does. It holds you in place so I can heal you."

When a Doctor places a caste on a broken arm, that caste does not instantaneously heal the broken arm. The caste must be worn for 6-8 weeks to give the body time to heal itself. The same thing is true about forgiveness and healing. We can forgive someone immediately but the pain may take a while to heal. Just because the pain still exists does not mean the person has not forgiven the person that hurt them.

Forgiveness starts the healing process but that healing process may take some time. Many people start this process but when it gets too difficult or painful they put a stop to the healing process. Stopping this process only means that you will live in the mess even longer. I know it may be the hardest thing you will ever do but it will be the most beneficial thing you can do as well. Do not stop this healing process! God only wants the best for you and sometimes going through the pain to get to the other side of it is the best thing.

Forgiveness and trust are two very different things. Just because you forgive someone does not mean that you should trust them. Forgiveness is a choice that you make and it is freely given because that is what Jesus tells us to do but trust must be earned. Forgiveness is about you and your healing but trust is about the other person. If the person, or, in my case, an institution, is not willing to change then trust cannot be earned.

This is where repentance comes into the picture. Repentance is about "turning away" from the wrong that was done. This means much more than just saying "I'm sorry". Repentance means the person that committed the wrong must stop doing the thing that hurt the person that was hurt. If there is not true repentance then trust cannot be developed. For relationships to be healthy and whole, both sides MUST do their part. If you forgive the person that hurt you but they have not repented then if you trust that person, you will get hurt again. If the person that hurt you has truly repented but you harden your heart and do not forgive then the relationship is damaged as well. Both sides must do their parts equally yet most Churches teach forgiveness but not as many Churches teach true repentance.

Another thing that many people told me through this healing process was that I was not supposed to take on a "spirit of offense". But this was not a "spirit of offense", these were deep wounds that had been inflicted on me by the Church and I was bleeding on them because of that pain and they did not know how to handle it.

I do believe that people can become offended and open themselves up to a "spirit of offense" but not everyone who has experienced a hurt has opened themselves up to a "spirit of offense". So, what is the difference between being offended and being hurt? The difference is in the willingness to forgive. People who take on a "spirit of offense" are not willing to forgive.

People who have been deeply hurt yet have chosen to forgive may not be healed yet and this pain can look like a "spirit of offense". What most people could not see or were not willing to see was that I had already made the choice to forgive these Pastors but I had not been healed of the pain yet. So, they assumed it was a "spirit of offense" in me. When we define the difference between deep hurt and "spirit of offense" in this way, then it means we must get to know the person that has been hurt to know whether they have forgiven or are willing to forgive. Most of the Christians that said this to me were not willing to truly get to know me to know if what they said was true or not. Also, when we tell hurting people that they have taken on a "spirit of offense", we are essentially blaming them for their own pain. It is time for us to stop blaming the victims of Church hurt for their own pain and start accepting responsibility for the mistakes we make as a Church and try to correct those mistakes.

Chapter 13: To Those Who Have Been Hurt in the Church

But choosing to forgive is only the first step in the healing process. The rest of the process is different for every person but essentially it means allowing God to take the anger and hurt and transform it into peace and joy. How does this happen? This can happen in many ways. Every person is unique and God works with each person differently but that is why God is so amazing. He can heal us in a way that is best for us.

When we get hurt we can become angry and that is very natural. God showed me an illustration of my hurt by giving me a picture of a dog that had been caught by the leg in an old-fashioned bear trap. That bear trap had mangled the dog's leg and the dog was slowly bleeding to death. The dog needed to be freed and the wound cared for or it would die in that trap. But every time someone would try to get close to the dog, he would snap and growl and try to bite people. He did this because he was afraid of being hurt even more. Because of the loss of blood, the rescuers could not use any tranquilizers on the hurting dog without causing more damage. So how do they help the dog? Someone would need to care enough about the dog to get close enough to free the dog. The person that would do this would be risking getting bitten but the risk was worth it.

For me, this healing process happened through a very dear friend that saw past the hurt and the anger and was willing to listen until he understood my hurt to the best of his ability. His name was TJ and he was willing to risk getting bitten to free me from the trap of my hurt and anger. We had met in my first year at ORU. We had been in science class together. At first, he was just another kid in my class but during the second year I was at school he stopped me one day to ask a question.

He asked me, "You're married, right?"

I nodded and then he asked, "So how do you know if it is the "right one"?

I laughed and started to tell him how I met Dean, my husband. I told him, "I can't exactly tell you how you will know, you will just know." For those of you that are married and a bit older, you will understand what I meant.

That started our friendship and he would come over to hang out with Dean and I a few times and even treated us to a dinner at a restaurant. We became friends but we weren't very close friends until after Dean died. TJ is 17 years younger than me and I saw him as a kid brother. Dean also liked him.

Before Dean died I was very careful about my friendships with other men. I was Dean's third wife and his first two wives had cheated on him so I knew I had to be very careful to not make him think I was also cheating on him. Consequently, I kept my friendships with other men at arm's length. So, I would see TJ in class and we would chat at lunch or he would hang out with both Dean and I but it was only a surface friendship for a long time. We graduated with our Bachelor's in 2012 and TJ went back to his home state of Connecticut. I did not think that I would see him again.

I was still hurting and I wrote this Facebook post on February 15, 2013:

Amy Leigh Moore
15 February 2013
A Plea for Love

What happens when you have nothing left to give?
Is there anyone that will give to me?
I feel so alone and adrift.
Will someone throw me a life preserver?
Because I feel as if I am drowning in this pain
I have lost the only one that I truly loved
And I am silently screaming for someone to care
I gave all that I had and am to that man
I have nothing left to give
But I am still asked to give
I am told to "give without expecting anything in return"
How can that be right?
Isn't love giving and taking?
Will someone give to me without expecting anything from me right away?
I need to heal before I can give
I want to give but right now I can't
Yet no one cares enough to give me that healing balm
They ask of me but no one cares enough to hold me while I cry
They tell me that only God can heal this deep of a pain
But I need human arms around me
Some have told me that my pain is too deep
They don't know how to help
I will tell you how
Just love me!!!!
Have been told that I come across as attacking and angry
I am hurting!
When a dog is caught in a trap and deeply wounded

Chapter 13: To Those Who Have Been Hurt in the Church

You don't tell that dog to stop snapping at people
He is just defending himself and people understand that
A person that wants to help will soothe and love the dog
Until they can get close enough to tend the dog's wounds
Why won't anyone soothe and love me?
Instead, I am told that I come across as angry
And people don't want to be around an angry person
I am not angry!
I'm deeply wounded just like the dog!
Why do they care more for a wounded dog then they do for me?
Don't love me because you want something from me
Just love me!
Love gives….it doesn't take!
For nine years, I gave
For three of those years, I begged someone to give to me!
No one other than my husband did!
He gave what he could but he was the needy one
I gave everything I had to him
And I pleaded for someone to give to me!
But groceries were more important than me
A renovation project was more important than me
Money was more important than me
And I am still asked to give!
Come to this meeting or this service
I am still supposed to give
I have nothing left!!
I need someone to give to me
And help me heal
Before I can give!
Please?

This post expresses all the pain and anguish I was feeling at the time. I think this may also express the pain other people feel from Church Hurt as well. Not long after I wrote that post, God brought TJ back into my life in a more meaningful way. His plans in Connecticut had fallen through and he came back to ORU to start on a

Master's degree. TJ had also dealt with his own personal tragedy and he sought me out to try to understand how to deal with it. This brought us closer together and as I helped him deal with his pain, he was open to hearing about mine.

TJ is a remarkable young man. Instead of instantly jumping to conclusions about me or misjudging me, he truly listened to me and tried to understand. He became a shoulder I could cry on and he didn't turn away from me because he felt uncomfortable about my pain. He also did not run away when I would get angry. He did not necessarily agree with my views on the Church but he listened with an open heart and truly tried to understand my pain. That helped me more than anything else could have. Many times, I did not need someone to "fix" the problem or try to "fix" me but to just listen and be a shoulder I could cry on. That was all I really was looking for from the Church as well.

In 2014, TJ moved back to his home state for good but we kept in contact via phone and Facebook. One day in the summer of 2014, TJ called me and told me that he felt God was telling him he was to start up a new Church and he wanted me to help him with it. I was very flattered and after a lot of prayer I told him I would help.

One of the things TJ asked me to do in preparation for this Church was to create a leadership-training curriculum. I was a bit overwhelmed by that project so I was a bit slow in getting started but once I started it everything just flowed out of me. Most of what you read in this book came out of that time of putting together that leadership-training curriculum.

As I studied and put together the outline, it was like God brought all the pieces together for me and I truly understood what God meant when He said the responsibility of the leader is to "watch out for the souls of the people". What TJ and I developed together is a revolutionary new way of "doing Church"! It is not in existence just yet but I am positive that in God's timing, it will become a reality!

TJ did one other thing for me that helped me more than he will ever truly know. One day, after I had finished the leadership-training curriculum, he called me and told me something I will treasure till my last dying breath. He said, "Amy, I see you as a hidden treasure. God has given you incredible insight but no one has taken the time to learn what that insight is. I feel privileged to be the one to be able to help uncover this hidden treasure!"

Even now, that still brings tears to my eyes and as far as I am concerned, TJ is the best little brother anyone could ever have. He has become a dear friend and a confidant and I love him dearly! God used him to heal my hurt more than anyone else because he

Chapter 13: To Those Who Have Been Hurt in the Church

was willing to get growled at and possibly bitten to help free me from my trap of anger and hurt.

There was one other person in my life that God used to help my healing process and that person was my sister-in-law Rhonda. We had not been very close while Dean was alive but after Dean died we became very close. She lived and still lives in North Carolina and I live in Tulsa but we spent many hours on the phone crying together and she helped me to make sense of all the stuff I had been through.

Rhonda would help me see what God's plans for me were and she even supported me financially when she could while I was in school. She is disabled but she would send me money when she could and that helped me very much. She is closer to me then my own sisters are and I also love her dearly.

Through the unconditional love and acceptance these people showed me, God started to put me back together again. The process has not been an easy or a quick one. So, for those of you reading this, I want you to know, God can heal your pain, just as He healed mine. Just don't give up on your faith and don't bury your pain. For God to be able to heal you, the pain must rise to the surface like oil rises above water. That way God can whisk away the pain quicker. When you bury the pain, and try to pretend it is not there, it will make the healing process harder and it will prolong the process. Even if it is the most painful thing in the world, continue to allow Him to do what He needs to do.

When I was healing from the sexual abuse from my childhood, I was living with my mother in 1999 and it was a healing time for both of us. But it was not an easy process. I remember one time that my mom and I were fighting and I do not have the foggiest idea over what and we were crying our eyes out. We were on the way to Church during this fight and when we pulled into the parking lot we looked at each other and mom said, "Do you really want to walk into the Church with tear stains on our cheeks?" I laughed and shook my head and we turned around and went back home.

Dealing with all this baggage was very hard on me. I felt like I was being torn to shreds on the inside and I remember one night in which I screamed at God, "I HAVE HAD ENOUGH! I CAN'T DEAL WITH THIS ANYMORE!"

I cried myself to sleep that night. While I was sleeping, God gave me a dream I will never forget. In the dream, I saw a ticker like one you would see on wall street. Instead of stock quotes it was scrolling a Scripture.

***Jeremiah 29:11** "For I know the plans I have for you," declares the Lord, "plans to prosper you and not to harm you, plans to give you hope and a future." NIV*

When the ticker got to the words "not to harm you" it stopped and started blinking in a bright neon red color. I instantly knew God was telling me to hold on for just a bit longer and not to put a stop to what was happening because it was painful. He was not trying to hurt me but to heal me.

The next morning, I decided to continue to let God do whatever He needed to do in me no matter how difficult it was. Within only a matter of a couple of weeks, I was free and I felt at peace. How did God do it? I have no idea but I don't need to know how He did it. All I need to know is that He did. I felt as if a vise grip had been taken off my brain and for the first time in my life I could think clearly and logically. I went back to school after this healing process and I maintained a 3.7 GPA over two years while working full time. This was a miracle for me because I barely graduated from high school with C's and D's and I failed out of college the first time around. My relationship with my mother was also healed through this process. I am very thankful for that because a few years later she passed away.

God is like a master surgeon and He will cut out the ugly tumors in our lives if we let Him do it. Sometimes we go through some very painful things and we don't understand why we go through those things. But I believe those hurts are God's way of cutting out the tumors in our lives. A cancer surgeon must use a knife to cut out the tumor and it may hurt like hell when he does it. But he is doing it to make you better and not to hurt you. If the surgeon did not cut out the tumor, then that tumor will kill you. God does the same thing. He must cut things out of our lives that will harm us and it may be very painful when He does this but He is doing it for our own good!

I can now say that I am glad I went through the deep Church hurt that I went through.

***James 1:2-4** "My brethren, count it all joy when you fall into various trials, 3 knowing that the testing of your faith produces patience. 4 But let patience have its perfect work, that you may be perfect and complete, lacking nothing."*

Just as James said, I can count it all joy now because what I have been through has made me into the person I am today. I am much more compassionate and patient with hurting people and I am much more willing to listen. If I had not gone through the pain I did, then I would not be the kind of person I am today. God has really turned

Chapter 13: To Those Who Have Been Hurt in the Church

what was meant for bad into something good in my life and He can do the same for you.

Also, I want people to understand that God and the Church are not the same thing. The Church is made up of imperfect people that have their own insecurities and hurts to deal with. And most Pastors do not have a complete understanding of what their responsibility is so they may inadvertently hurt people through that lack of knowledge. God is perfect and has perfect knowledge and will never hurt you. He may ask you to go through some painful things but His purpose is always to heal you and to bring you hope and a future!

So, allow God to take you through the healing process and when you get to the other side, He can use you to help other people heal. Once you are healed then you can turn around and help to free other hurting people become free from their own bear traps. And God needs more people willing to risk getting bitten so He can heal their wounds like He healed mine. You may be the person that God uses to implement the strategies I outlined in the rest of this book to build the Church on a complete foundation so less people get hurt in the Church. But to do so, you must be healed of your own pain first.

Amy Leigh Moore

Conclusion

Stop the Insanity

If the Church is to preserve our society and start being the salt of the earth, then the Church must do something different. It is obvious that what the Church is doing now is not preserving our world. If we would build the Church on a complete foundation, then I believe the saltiness would come back into our Church and we would start to do Church in the Jesus way instead of in the consumer way. The world would look at us and say the same thing they said about the Church in Acts. Tertullian reported that the Romans would exclaim, "See how they love one another!" When they see our love then we can start to preserve the world just like salt preserves meat.

Matthew 5:13 "You are the salt of the earth; but if the salt loses its flavor, how shall it be seasoned? It is then good for nothing but to be thrown out and trampled underfoot by men."

One of my favorite quotes is the definition of insanity by Albert Einstein. "Insanity: doing the same thing over and over again and expecting different results." So, if we want to see different results we need to do things differently.

The Church has split into many different denominations and they may have changed some surface things such as the type of music that is played or the type of seating in the sanctuary but the one thing they haven't changed is the foundation of the Church. Thus, millions of people have been hurt in the Church. Since a couple of generations after Jesus' disciples left this earth for Heaven, the Church has lost its main goal and mission: to make disciples and meet the needs of the people just a shepherd meets the needs of his flock.

Every person in ministry believes their responsibility is to reach as many people as possible with the Gospel of Jesus and I believe that as well. But what good does it do to tell people that Jesus loves them if we don't provide for all their needs, not just their Spiritual needs? The best way to show the love of Jesus and thus spread the Gospel is by meeting all the needs of the people. When we finally put the needs of the people ahead of the needs of the ministry then we will see true revival and power come back into the

Church. By doing Church in this way we can also prevent a lot of people from being hurt.

Many people have left the Church and one of the main reasons that is given is a lack of "realness" in the Church. People are not looking for empty rituals but for people that will truly care about them without judging them by appearances. What they are looking for is the kind of sacrificial love that Jesus commanded we show to one another. The reason people (especially the younger generations) are leaving is because they do not see true love in the Church. Many Pastors think the younger generation is looking for flashier light shows and modern music but that is not at all what they want. They want to see a Jesus that is real and that will not sugar coat things and is honest. They want a Jesus that loves them in action and not just in words. They want a Jesus that will care for ALL their needs instead of just giving lip service to caring for their souls. They want a leader who is humble enough to admit when they have made mistakes and try to fix those mistakes. We need to start being that type of Church.

I have also heard many people say that the Church is no longer relevant to our modern way of life. What a better way to correct that problem then to create a Church in which the main goal is to meet the needs of the people through love and relationships in the same way a shepherd takes care of the needs of his flock! If we would build our Churches on this foundation, then the Church would become very relevant to our society.

I would love to be part of a Church that would put the needs of the people ahead of the needs of the building or the ministry, like a shepherd would put the needs of the flock ahead of his own needs. As far as I know, there is no Church anywhere that is doing that. This book is not intended to be a complete manual about how to do that but, rather, it is a foundation on which Church leaders can build and develop their own ideas on how to accomplish this huge mission. These are ideas that I believe God has given me on how to fulfill this massive responsibility but these ideas are only ideas on paper and have not been put into practice just yet. Because of that, I do not know what the actual results of doing something like this will be. Ideas on paper rarely look the same in practice. Because of this, I would love to work with a Pastoral staff somewhere who would be willing to try these ideas and come up with some of their own. If this book has touched you and you would like to try some of these ideas and would like my help, you can contact me at amoore41302@yahoo.com.

So, my final thought is this: Let's be the type of Church God is really looking for and let's stop the insanity!

Loving By Faith Bible Study

The first step in changing the Church to better fit what the Scriptures say the Church should be is learning how to love. Our Pastors preach "Love the Lord your God with all you heart and Love your neighbor as you love yourself" but they don't teach the people how to do it. Preaching the "what" without teaching the "how" is pointless. So, I have developed a small groups Bible Study that will teach people how to love by faith. This Bible Study is a more in-depth look, into the concepts I introduced in Chapter 8 of this book.

Week 1
- What is Faith?

I. **The Just shall live by Faith.**

A. Habakkuk 2:4 "Behold the proud, His soul is not upright in him; But the just shall live by his faith."

B. Galatians 3:11 "But that no one is justified by the law in the sight of God is evident, for "the just shall live by faith.""

C. Romans 1:17 "For in it the righteousness of God is revealed from faith to faith; as it is written, "The just shall live by faith.""

D. Hebrews 10:38 "Now the just shall live by faith; But if anyone draws back, My soul has no pleasure in him."

II. What is faith?

A. Mark 5:25-34 "Now a certain woman had a flow of blood for twelve years, ²⁶and had suffered many things from many physicians. She had spent all that she had and was no better, but rather grew worse. ²⁷When she heard about Jesus, she came behind Him in the crowd and touched His garment. ²⁸For she said, "If only I may touch His clothes, I shall be made well." ²⁹Immediately the fountain of her blood was dried up, and she felt in her body that she was healed of the affliction. ³⁰And Jesus, immediately knowing in Himself that power had gone out of Him, turned around in the crowd and said, "Who touched My clothes?" ³¹But His disciples said to Him, "You see the multitude thronging You, and You say, 'Who touched Me?'" ³²And He looked around to see her who had done this thing. ³³But the woman, fearing and trembling, knowing what had happened to her, came and fell down before Him and told Him the whole truth. ³⁴And He said to her, "Daughter, your faith has made you well. Go in peace, and be healed of your affliction.""

1. What were her physical symptoms? Loss of blood causes anemia. Symptoms of anemia from webmd.com include:

    a. Easy fatigue and loss of energy

    b. Unusually rapid heartbeat, particularly with exercise

    c. Shortness of breath and headache, particularly with exercise

    d. Difficulty concentrating

    e. Dizziness

    f. Leg cramps

    g. Insomnia

    h. A tingling, "pins and needles" sensation in the hands or feet

    i. Lost sense of touch

    j. A wobbly gait and difficulty walking

    k. Clumsiness and stiffness of the arms and legs

    l. Dementia

    m. Hallucinations, paranoia, and schizophrenia

    n. Weakened immune system

2. Cultural and Legal Issues for this woman in Jewish Society

    a. Leviticus 15:25-28 "'If a woman has a discharge of blood for many days, other than at the time of her customary impurity, or if it runs beyond her usual time of impurity, all the days of her unclean discharge shall be as the days of her customary impurity. She shall be unclean. ²⁶Every bed on which she lies all the days of her discharge shall be to her as the bed of her impurity; and whatever she sits on shall be unclean, as the uncleanness of her impurity. ²⁷Whoever touches those things shall be unclean; he shall wash his clothes and bathe in water, and be unclean until evening. ²⁸'But if she is cleansed of her discharge, then she shall count for herself seven days, and after that she shall be clean."

b. She would have been an outcast in her own society because she was constantly bleeding.

c. According to her culture, she was not to approach anyone, especially a Rabbi who was ceremoniously clean. Just by touching His clothes, she would have made Him unclean. On top of that, she was a woman. Why would a menstruating woman be unclean? According to Old Testament Law, a person must be ritualistically clean to be able to approach God. The physical condition needed to approach God was interpreted as "the fullness of life." If something or someone was full of life then it or they were deemed clean and then could approach God. So, a woman who was menstruating was unable to bear life and was therefore unclean.

3. What did the Doctors do for her?

  a. Bloodletting

  b. Purging or vomiting

  c. Rubbing with rocks or herbs

  d. Sweating

  e. Starvation

  f. Bath in vinegar

  g. An enema

  h. Frankincense and myrrh

  i. The opening to her vagina would have been sewed shut

These remedies would have made her worse off just as verse 26 states

4. What did all this do to her emotionally?

  a. Hopelessness – Put yourself in her shoes and imagine going from doctor to doctor for twelve years and going broke in the process and only to be worse not better

b. Loneliness – Because of her culture she would have been isolated because she was viewed as unclean. No one wanted to be friends with someone who was unclean.

c. Depression – The loneliness and the hopelessness would have resulted in deep depression. I could imagine that at times, she would have wanted to die.

5. What did she do?

   a. But she did not give up!

   b. She said repeatedly that if she could just touch His cloak then she would be healed. These words spurred her to action.

   c. She believed that the stories about Jesus being a healer and having compassion on the sick were true.

   d. She had heard where Jesus would be and made sure she was there when He was.

   e. She was heavily cloaked so no one would recognize her and send her away before she could accomplish the task she had set out to do.

   f. She was totally determined and she fought a large crowd to get to Jesus, despite her weakness.

   g. She was successful!

   h. When Jesus asked who had touched Him, she had the courage to admit what she had done, even though it could have caused her punishment and death.

6. What were the results?

   a. She felt the strength return to her body and she also felt that her bleeding had stopped

   b. She was healed of the emotional problems caused by the illness

   c. She received the eventual restoration of her reputation and wealth.

   d. The reason for my belief in total restoration is the word that was translated 'whole' in Mark 5:28 and 34. According to the Strong's Greek Dictionary, this word is sozo in the Greek and can also mean "to make whole" or "save". This implies that she went after and received more than just her physical healing. She received salvation in the spiritual as well as the physical.

    e. Jesus was an observer in this story, just as you and I are. He even told her that it was HER FAITH that made her WHOLE!

B. The definition of Faith.

1. By studying this story, I have developed a definition of faith that is very practical and can be used in everyday life so that the "just shall live by faith".

2. The definition of faith is "A conscious decision to believe what the Bible says is true despite what our feelings say or our circumstances say and then acting on that decision"

3. This definition has two parts

    a. First, we must make a conscious decision to believe that what God's Word says is true. If we won't do that then there is no reason to move on to the next step because it won't work

    b. Secondly, we must act on that decision. James 2:20 "But do you want to know, O foolish man, that faith without works is dead?" But if we believe and don't act on that belief then our faith won't work either.

III. A Modern-Day Example of Faith

A. Most of us work jobs. We believe that if we work so many hours per week, we will get paid a certain amount

B. We must work the required number of hours BEFORE we get our pay

C. We get out of bed and go to work, even when we don't feel like it

D. We have faith in our employer that if we work the required number of hours we will get paid a certain amount of money

E. Faith in God works the same way. God says believe what I say and then act on that belief and you will receive what He promises you will receive

We have more faith in our employer then we do in God!

Loving by Faith Journal

Week 1

The Bible is full of the promises of God. But every one of those promises require faith for them to come true in your life. Many of those promises are written in an "if, then" format. God says "if" you will do this "then" I will do that. One of my favorite promises is John 15:7 "If you abide in Me, and My words abide in you, you will ask what you desire, and it shall be done for you."

Notice the prerequisite in this promise is that we must abide in Jesus and His Words must abide in us. This means that we must be studying the Bible for ourselves and not relying on the Pastor's sermons. If we study the Bible for ourselves then God promises us that we can ask whatever we want and He will do it for us! What an amazing promise! But to receive this promise we must first believe that it is true and then act on that belief by doing what this verse says to do and study the Bible for ourselves!

There are many more promises that God gives us in Scripture. I suggest that you do a Google search for God's promises and find one that applies to your life. Then describe your feelings about this promise. Do you truly believe that this is true? If so, then how will you act on that belief? Please describe how you have acted on the belief that God's promise is true.

Loving By Faith Bible Study

Week 2

- How do we "love by faith"?

I. Life without love is empty. Loving is part of living so if we are to live by faith we must also love by faith.

   A. Matthew 22:37-39 "You shall love the LORD your God with all your heart, with all your soul, and with all your mind. This is the first and great commandment. And the second is like it: you shall love your neighbor as yourself."

      1. How many steps are seen in the above verses? Most people would say two but there are four.

      2. A person cannot love God until she firmly believes that He loves her. 1 John 4:19 says, "We love Him because He first loved us." People also cannot love their neighbors unless they fully love themselves.

      3. When we incorporate the above definition of faith into these steps we can see that these four steps are:

        a. Make a conscious decision to believe that God loves you.
        b. Make a conscious decision to love Him in the same way that He loves you.
        c. Make a conscious decision to love yourself as God loves you.
        d. Make a conscious decision to love your neighbor as you love yourself.

   B. Once you make these conscious decisions then you must act on those decisions.

      1. We act on the decision to believe that God loves us by keeping His commandments.

        a. John 15:9-10 "As the Father loved Me, I also have loved you; abide in My love. If you keep My commandments, you will abide in My love, just as I have kept My Father's commandments and abide in His love."

        b. When we keep God's commandments then we are acting on the belief of His love for us.

      2. We act on the decision to love God by putting Him first in our lives.

        a. God told Abraham to leave everything he knew and to go to a place which God would tell him. Genesis 12:1-4 "Now the Lord had said to

Abram: "Get out of your country, from your family and from your father's house, to a land that I will show you. I will make you a great nation; I will bless you and make your name great; and you shall be a blessing. I will bless those who bless you, and I will curse him who curses you; and in you all the families of the earth shall be blessed." So, Abram departed as the Lord had spoken to him, and Lot went with him. And Abram was seventy-five years old when he departed from Haran." Abram loved God so much that he put God first and left his entire family behind to go to a land that he knew nothing about. His nephew Lot and his wife were the only family to go with him.

b. Jesus also gave us a promise if we love God enough to leave everything else behind. Mark 10:29-30 "So Jesus answered and said, "Assuredly, I say to you, there is no one who has left house or brothers or sisters or father or mother or wife or children or lands, for My sake and the gospel's, who shall not receive a hundredfold now in this time—houses and brothers and sisters and mothers and children and lands, with persecutions—and in the age to come, eternal life." Notice He says we will receive a hundred-fold in return but in this life that hundred-fold will come with persecution. But by doing so we will receive eternal life in Heaven. In Heaven, there will be no persecution.

c. Jesus also showed us how He loved the Father by putting the Father's will above His own will. Matthew 26:38-39 "Then He said to them, "My soul is exceedingly sorrowful, even to death. Stay here and watch with Me." He went a little farther and fell on His face, and prayed, saying, "O My Father, if it is possible, let this cup pass from Me; nevertheless, not as I will, but as You will." Jesus was in agony over the knowledge of what He was about to go through but He loved God and us more than He loved Himself and thus He put what the Father wanted above what He wanted.

3. We act on the decision to love ourselves by sacrificially doing what is best for ourselves.

a. 1 Corinthians 6:19-20 "Or do you not know that your body is the temple of the Holy Spirit who is in you, whom you have from God, and you are not your own? For you were bought at a price; therefore, glorify God in your body and in your spirit, which are God's."

b. If we are to love ourselves that means we must sacrificially put our needs before our wants. This means that we live a disciplined life and do what is best for ourselves, even if it is not what we want. We need to eat right and exercise, stop smoking and stop expecting instance gratification. These are the things that are best for us and if we are to truly love ourselves then we must do what is best for ourselves.

4. We act on the decision to love others as we love ourselves by putting the needs of others ahead of our own needs.

a. John 13:34-35 "A new commandment I give to you, that you love one another; as I have loved you, that you also love one another. By this all will know that you are My disciples, if you have love for one another."

b. Notice that Jesus said this BEFORE he died on the cross. So how did He love his disciples besides dying for them? He cared enough about them to get to know them and to place their needs above his own. He spent almost 24 hours a day for three years with these men and put up with their lack of faith and their bickering because He loved them.

c. Jesus even made sure the taxes were paid for Peter and Himself. Matthew 17:24-27 "When they had come to Capernaum, those who received the temple tax came to Peter and said, "Does your Teacher not pay the temple tax?" He said, "Yes." And when he had come into the house, Jesus anticipated him, saying, "What do you think, Simon? From whom do the kings of the earth take customs or taxes, from their sons or from strangers?" Peter said to Him, "From strangers." Jesus said to him, "Then the sons are free. Nevertheless, lest we offend them, go to the sea, cast in a hook, and take the fish that comes up first. And when you have opened its mouth, you will find a piece of money; take that and give it to them for Me and you."

Amy Leigh Moore

Loving by Faith Journal

Week 2

Choose **ONE** of the steps of love and discuss how you feel about that step, what God may have shown you regarding that step and how you will incorporate that step into your life.

1. Make a conscious decision to believe that God loves you and act on that decision by keeping His commandments.

2. Make a conscious decision to love Him in the same way that He loves you and act on that decision by putting Him first in your life.

3. Make a conscious decision to love yourself as God loves you and act on that decision by sacrificially doing what is best for yourself.

4. Make a conscious decision to love your neighbor as you love yourself and act on that decision by putting the needs of others ahead of your own needs.

Amy Leigh Moore

Week 3

Love is Patient

I. If we are to love by faith, then we need to understand what love is.

   A. To understand what love is we must look at 1 Corinthians 13:4-8a "Love is patient, love is kind. It does not envy, it does not boast, it is not proud. It does not dishonor others, it is not self-seeking, it is not easily angered, and it keeps no record of wrongs. Love does not delight in evil but rejoices with the truth. It always protects, always trusts, always hopes, and always perseveres. Love never fails."

   B. Each week we will examine each aspect of love in these verses and apply the four-step process to each aspect.

II. This week we will look at patience. 1 Corinthians 13:4 says that love is patient. Another way to say this is that love equals patience.

   A. So, what exactly is patience?

   1. HELPS Word-studies defines patience as the Greek word *hypomonḗ* (from *hypó*, "under" and *ménō*, "remain, endure") – properly, remaining under, endurance; steadfastness, especially as God enables the believer to "remain (endure) under" the challenges He allots in life.

   2. Thayer's Greek Lexicon defines patience as

       a. steadfastness, constancy, endurance - the characteristic of a man who is un-swerved from his deliberate purpose and his loyalty to faith and piety by even the greatest trials and sufferings

       b. a patient, steadfast waiting for; expectation, hope

       c. a patient enduring, sustaining

   3. Strong's Exhaustive Concordance defines patience as the Greek word *hypomonḗ* - cheerful (or hopeful) endurance, constancy -- enduring, patience, patient continuance (waiting).

   4. The definition of patient in Webster's Dictionary is:

a. Bearing pain or trials without complaint,

   b. Showing self-control: Calm,

   c. Steadfast despite opposition difficulty or adversity, perseverance.

   5. So, to put this all together we can say that patience means to endure with a hopeful and expectant and calm waiting for something or someone despite all opposition, difficulties, or adversities.

B. Let's apply the four-step process we learned last week to patience.

   1. Make a conscious decision to believe that God is patient with you and then act on that decision.

      a. 2 Peter 3:9 "The Lord is not slow in keeping his promise, as some understand slowness. Instead he is patient with you, not wanting anyone to perish, but everyone to come to repentance." God endures with a hopeful and expectant and calm waiting for us to come to repentance or to turn away from our sin.

      b. Philippians 1:6 "being confident of this very thing, that He who has begun a good work in you will complete it until the day of Jesus Christ;" God will complete the work He started in you and He is patient in seeing that work completed. We must make a conscious decision to believe this. But how do we act on it?

      c. Hebrews 12:1-2 "Therefore we also, since we are surrounded by so great a cloud of witnesses, let us lay aside every weight, and the sin which so easily ensnares us, and let us run with endurance the race that is set before us, looking unto Jesus, the author and finisher of our faith, who for the joy that was set before Him endured the cross, despising the shame, and has sat down at the right hand of the throne of God."

      d. We lay aside or turn away from or repent of our sin and look to Jesus because He endured the cross for us. How do we look to Jesus? Study the Bible daily and communicate with Him regularly. This is how we act on our belief that God is patient with us.

   2. Make a conscious decision to be patient with God and then act on that decision.

a. Isaiah 40:31 "But those who wait on the Lord shall renew their strength; they shall mount up with wings like eagles, they shall run and not be weary, they shall walk and not faint.

b. We must wait for God's timing in our lives because His timing is perfect. The word "wait" in the Hebrew is "quavah" which means (probably originally twist, stretch, then of tension of enduring, waiting) wait, cord; be strong, strength, also strand of rope; endure, remain, await, or threads.

c. I like the "strand of rope" definition. Imagine the process of making a rope. The threads of the rope are twisted or bound together to form the rope. The more strands that are twisted or woven together in a rope, the greater is its strength. When a rope lifts or pulls a load, it stretches a little while it is working. As it stretches, the individual strands are pulled closer together. While this "stress" is on the rope, the individual strands work together to lift or pull the load. No one individual strand does all the work. If it did, it would snap. A rope's strength comes from all the strands working together. When we are waiting on the Lord we should be building our ropes or binding our ropes together because after the waiting period is over we will be putting those ropes to work and the more strands that rope has the stronger it becomes. So, what are the strands that make up our ropes? Knowledge of God's Word is a major strand as is regular communication with Jesus. Godly friends are another strand. (I do not use the word Church because I personally have not found many Godly friends in Church).

d. 1 Peter 5:6-7 "Therefore humble yourselves under the mighty hand of God, that He may exalt you in due time, casting all your care upon Him, for He cares for you." Another strand in our rope is humility. When we humble ourselves enough to be willing to wait on God's timing that just adds one more strand to the strength of our rope.

e. So, we must decide to be patient with God and wait on His timing and the way we act on that decision is to build or bind our ropes up to prepare for the task ahead. We build our ropes by spending time for ourselves in God's Word and talk to God daily. Godly friends can also help to build our ropes; as does humility.

f. When we do these things, God promises to give us strength and that we will soar with the eagles. He also promises to exalt us when the time is right.

3. Make a conscious decision to be patient with yourself and then act on that decision.

a. One of the definitions of patience is to bear pain or trials without complaint. We will go through pains and trials and if we deal with them correctly they will produce patience in us.

b. Romans 5:3-5 "And not only that, but we also glory in tribulations, knowing that tribulation produces perseverance; and perseverance, character; and character, hope. Now hope does not disappoint, because the love of God has been poured out in our hearts by the Holy Spirit who was given to us."

c. Sometimes we beat ourselves up and lose patience with ourselves when we don't do what we know we should do. How many times have you thought in your head, "I am such an idiot! Why did I do that?"

d. When we lose patience with ourselves we open the door for Satan to condemn us. Condemnation is not from God and condemnation will cause us to stop moving forward.

e. Romans 8:1 "There is therefore now no condemnation to those who are in Christ Jesus, who do not walk according to the flesh, but according to the Spirit." Even when we walk in the Spirit we are going to make mistakes. So instead of losing patience with yourself and allowing condemnation into your thoughts, ask God to forgive you, forgive yourself and move forward.

4. Make a conscious decision to be patient with other people and then act on that decision.

a. Again, I turn to the definition of patience that says to bear pain or trials without complaint. We automatically think that means our own pain and trials but it also means other people's pain and trials.

b. Galatians 6:2 "Bear one another's burdens, and so fulfill the law of Christ." The Greek word for "bear" is "***bastazo***", which means to endure, declare, sustain, receive, etc. -- bear, carry, to take up. The picture that I see from this definition is a heavy burden that can't be carried alone so we must help the person carry that burden.

c. Sometimes bearing with people means we let them yell or cry or whatever they need to do to deal with the things they are going through and to be patient with them means we do this without complaint.

d. My friend TJ and my sister in law Rhonda were very patient with me through my healing process. Their willingness to bear my burdens with me is one of the things God used to help me heal.

Loving By Faith Bible Study

Loving by Faith Journal

Week 3

Choose **ONE** of the steps of patience and discuss how you feel about that step, what God may have shown you regarding that step and how you will incorporate that step into your life.

1. Make a conscious decision to believe that God is patient with you and then act on that decision.

2. Make a conscious decision to be patient with God and then act on that decision.

3. Make a conscious decision to be patient with yourself and then act on that decision.

4. Make a conscious decision to be patient with other people and then act on that decision.

Loving By Faith Bible Study

Week 4

Love is Kind

I. If we are to love by faith, then we need to understand what love is.

    A. To understand what love is we must look at 1 Corinthians 13:4-8a "Love is patient, love is kind. It does not envy, it does not boast, it is not proud. It does not dishonor others, it is not self-seeking, it is not easily angered, and it keeps no record of wrongs. Love does not delight in evil but rejoices with the truth. It always protects, always trusts, always hopes, and always perseveres. Love never fails."

    B. Each week we will examine each aspect of love in these verses and apply the four-step process to each aspect.

II. This week we will look at kindness. 1 Corinthians 13:4 says that love is kind or we can say that love equals kindness.

    A. What is the definition of kindness?

        1. HELPS Word-studies defines kindness as the Greek word *xrēstótēs* – properly, useable, i.e. well-fit for use (for what is really needed); kindness that is also serviceable.

        2. *xrēstótēs* ("useful kindness") refers to meeting real needs, in God's way, in His timing (fashion). Hence *xrēstótēs* is listed as a fruit of the Holy Spirit (Gal 5:22). With the believer, *xrēstótēs* ("divine kindness") is the Spirit-produced goodness which meets the need and avoids human harshness (cruelty). "We have no term that quite carries this notion of kind and good".

        3. xáris (another feminine noun from xar-, "favor, disposed to, inclined, favorable towards, leaning towards to share benefit") – properly, grace. (xáris) is preeminently used of the Lord's favor – freely extended to give Himself away to people (because He is "always leaning toward them").

        4. xáris ("grace") answers directly to the Hebrew (OT) term Kaná ("grace, extension-toward"). Both refer to God freely extending Himself (His favor, grace), reaching (inclining) to people because He is disposed to bless (be near) them.

5. So, we can define kindness by saying it is "reaching out to meet people's needs in a favorable and gracious way and without cruelty".

B. Now let's apply the four-step process to kindness.

1. Make a conscious decision to believe that God reaches out to you to meet your needs in a favorable and gracious way and without cruelty and act on that decision.

   a. Philippians 4:6 "Be anxious for nothing, but in everything by prayer and supplication, with thanksgiving, let your requests be made known to God."

   b. Philippians 4:19 "And my God shall supply all your need according to His riches in glory by Christ Jesus."

   c. Matthew 7:7 "Ask, and it will be given to you; seek, and you will find; knock, and it will be opened to you."

   d. John 15:7 "If you abide in Me, and My words abide in you, you will ask what you desire, and it shall be done for you."

   e. James 4:3 "You ask and do not receive, because you ask amiss, that you may spend it on your pleasures."

   f. Every one of these verses say that God will meet our needs but we must ask Him for that to happen. But we must ask for the right reasons and the right motives and do what God tells us to do for God to meet our needs. If we ask out of a motive of greed then God will not meet our greed.

2. Make a conscious decision to be kind to God and reach out to meet His needs and then act on that decision.

   a. God has needs that we can meet. Isaiah 66:1 "Thus says the Lord: "Heaven is My throne, And earth is My footstool. Where is the house that you will build Me? And where is the place of My rest?"

   b. In the Old Testament God resided in Heaven and would occasionally come down to earth to reside in the tabernacle or Temple that was built for Him.

c. But when Jesus died and rose again, He opened the way for God's home to be in our hearts. Ephesians 3:14-19 "For this reason I bow my knees to the Father of our Lord Jesus Christ, from whom the whole family in heaven and earth is named, that He would grant you, according to the riches of His glory, to be strengthened with might through His Spirit in the inner man, **that Christ may dwell in your hearts through faith**; that you, being rooted and grounded in love, may be able to comprehend with all the saints what is the width and length and depth and height— to know the love of Christ which passes knowledge; that you may be filled with all the fullness of God."

d. We also became the Temple of the Holy Spirit and He lives in us. 1 Corinthians 6:19-20 "Or do you not know that your body is the temple of the Holy Spirit who is in you, whom you have from God, and you are not your own? For you were bought at a price; therefore, glorify God in your body and in your spirit, which are God's."

e. So, God needs a home and through Jesus the home that God wants is in our hearts. So, to be kind to God means we must meet His need in a favorable and gracious way and without cruelty and God's need is for a home. When we open our hearts, and allow God to make his home in us then we are being kind to God.

3. Make a conscious decision to be kind to yourself and to meet your own needs and act on that decision.

   a. Ephesians 2:10 "For we are His workmanship, created in Christ Jesus for good works, which God prepared beforehand that we should walk in them." We are created by God so we should treat ourselves with the same type of kindness we treat God and other people with.

   b. Many people are very hard on themselves and try to hold themselves to a higher standard than they hold other people. When they don't live up to that standard, they beat themselves up and condemn themselves.

   c. Romans 8:1 "There is therefore now no condemnation to those who are in Christ Jesus, who do not walk according to the flesh, but according to the Spirit." When we allow Jesus to live in our hearts then we are in

Christ Jesus and therefore condemnation has no place in our lives. We all will make mistakes but when a mistake is made, repent, and move on.

d. When condemnation tries to enter your thoughts, reject it. What is condemnation? Thoughts such as "you are such an idiot" and "what is wrong with me" are thoughts of condemnation. Condemnation will make you feel like less of a person. On the other hand, God's conviction will say, "you made a mistake" or "that was the wrong thing to do". God's conviction will focus on what you did but condemnation will focus on who you are.

e. When we decide to be kind to ourselves, we will reject condemnation because it is cruel and unusual punishment. Even when we make mistakes, we should never be cruel to ourselves. We have a need to fix our mistakes but that can be done without being cruel to ourselves and condemning ourselves.

4. Make a conscious decision to be kind to other people and meet other people's needs and then act on that decision.

a. Ephesians 4:31-32 "Let all bitterness, wrath, anger, clamor, and evil speaking be put away from you, with all malice. And be kind to one another, tenderhearted, forgiving one another, even as God in Christ forgave you."

b. When we are kind to others, we are reaching out to meet people's needs in a favorable and gracious way and without cruelty. The first part of this definition states that we must reach out to meet people's needs. We can't meet their needs if we don't know what those needs are. So, the first thing we must do is care enough about other people to find out what they need. This means that we listen to them and go beyond the surface.

c. Secondly, this definition says we need to meet their need. Sometimes people have needs that can't be met through rules and regulations. We need to love people enough to think outside the box to meet their need if that is what is called for.

d. Thirdly, when we meet other people's need we should do so out of compassion and not treat them as if they were just a number and not a human being.

Amy Leigh Moore

Loving by Faith Journal

Week 4

Choose **ONE** of the steps of kindness and discuss how you feel about that step, what God may have shown you regarding that step and how you will incorporate that step into your life.

1. Make a conscious decision to believe that God reaches out to you to meet your needs in a favorable and gracious way and without cruelty and then act on that decision.

2. Make a conscious decision to be kind to God and then act on that decision.

3. Make a conscious decision to be kind to yourself and act on that decision.

4. Make a conscious decision to be kind to other people and then act on that decision.

Week 5

Love does not envy

I. If we are to love by faith, then we need to understand what love is.

   A. To understand what love is we must look at 1 Corinthians 13:4-8a "Love is patient, love is kind. It does not envy, it does not boast, it is not proud. It does not dishonor others, it is not self-seeking, it is not easily angered, and it keeps no record of wrongs. Love does not delight in evil but rejoices with the truth. It always protects, always trusts, always hopes, and always perseveres. Love never fails."

   B. Each week we will examine each aspect of love in these verses and apply the four-step process to each aspect.

II. This week we will look at envy or jealousy. When we love we are not to be envious or jealous.

   A. What is the definition of envy or jealousy?

      1. *Phthónos* – properly, strong feeling (desire) that sours, due to the influence of sin; (figuratively) the miserable trait of being glad when someone experiences misfortune or pain.

      2. *Phthónos* ("the feeling of ill-will") refers to the jealous envy that negatively "energizes" someone with an embittered mind. *Phthónos* ("ill-will") conveys "displeasure at another's good; . . . without longing to raise oneself to the level of him whom he envies, but only to depress the envied to his own level".

      3. The definition for jealousy is *zēlóō* – properly, to bubble over because so hot (boiling); "to burn with zeal"; "to be deeply committed to something, with the implication of accompanying desire – 'to be earnest, to set one's heart on, to be completely intent upon' ".

      4. The English word jealousy is defined as an unhappy or angry feeling of wanting to have what someone else has: an unhappy or angry feeling caused by the belief that someone you love (such as your husband or wife) likes or is liked by someone else

5. To put this all together Envy is an attitude of burning zeal that sours a person's soul because that person is glad when someone else experiences misfortune or pain or they want what someone else has.

6. Love does not have an attitude of burning zeal that sours their soul because they are glad when someone else experiences misfortune or pain or they want what someone else has.

B. Let's apply the four-step process to not being envious.

1. Make a conscious choice to believe that God is not glad when we experience misfortune or pain or that He wants what we have and then act on that decision.

   a. In John 11 we find the story of the death and resurrection of Lazarus. The shortest verse in the Bible is in this chapter because when Jesus saw how distressed Mary and Martha were, He wept. God weeps when we weep because He loves us so much that He feels our pain.

   b. Hebrews 4:15-16 "For we do not have a High Priest who cannot sympathize with our weaknesses, but was in all points tempted as we are, yet without sin. 16 Let us therefore come boldly to the throne of grace, that we may obtain mercy and find grace to help in time of need."

   c. Jesus is our High Priest and He understands our weaknesses and our pain. So, when we make a conscious decision to believe this then how we act on this decision is to go boldly to God is prayer and not be afraid that He will strike us dead if we say the wrong thing.

2. Make a conscious decision to not be glad when God experiences pain or to want what God has and then act on that decision.

   a. God can experience pain. Ephesians 4:30 "And do not grieve the Holy Spirit of God, by whom you were sealed for the day of redemption." If we are commanded to not grieve the Holy Spirit then that tells us that God can feel pain. Grief is a very painful experience and this verse tells us that God can grieve.

   b. We are not to be glad that God is grieved. When we sense that God may be grieved we should minister to Him through our worship. 1 Peter 2:9

"But you are a chosen generation, a royal priesthood, a holy nation, His own special people, that you may proclaim the praises of Him who called you out of darkness into His marvelous light."

c. I heard Jesse Duplantis speak on this one day. He stated that he felt God was grieved one day and that someone had hurt our Lord. So, he cancelled his appointments and started worshiping and praising God until God told him that he could go back to his day. How many of us think about putting God's needs for worship ahead of our own daily schedules?

d. Another aspect of envy is to crave what someone else has. How can we crave what God has? Satan craved what God had and that is why he was caste out of Heaven. Isaiah 14:12-14 "How you are fallen from heaven, O Lucifer, son of the morning! How you are cut down to the ground, you who weakened the nations! For you have said in your heart: 'I will ascend into heaven, I will exalt my throne above the stars of God; I will also sit on the mount of the congregation on the farthest sides of the north; I will ascend above the heights of the clouds, I will be like the Most High.' The way we prevent ourselves from craving what God has is to concentrate on how much He has given us and worship Him as a result.

e. So, what is worship? If how we act on the decision to not be envious of God is to worship Him then we must know what worship is.

i. *Proskynéō* – properly, to kiss the ground when prostrating before a superior; to worship, ready "to fall down/prostrate oneself to adore on one's knees"; to "do obeisance".

ii. *Proskyneō* has been (metaphorically) described as "the kissing-ground" between believers (the Bride) and Christ (the heavenly Bridegroom). While this is true, (*proskynéō*) suggests the willingness to make all necessary physical gestures of obeisance.

iii. So, to worship God means to prostrate ourselves before Him and make ourselves lower than He is; to lift Him up.

f. If we are to make a conscious decision to not be glad when God is grieved or to not crave what He has and act on that decision then we must be close enough to the Lord to sense when He is grieved and then worship Him. You do not have to be in a Church service to worship God. Some of the best worship experiences I have had have been when I have been all alone.

3. Make a conscious decision to not be glad when we experience pain and to not despise the good things in our lives and then act on that decision.

   a. The question that comes to my mind is how could we possibly be envious of ourselves? Well to answer that I want to ask another question: Have you ever been so happy that you thought it was too good to be true? Sometimes we think we are supposed to experience misfortune and pain and if we are not doing so then something is wrong. Some people revel in their pain and misery.

   b. Some people don't know how to accept God's best for themselves because they don't think they deserve it and thus they become envious of themselves. A Biblical example of this is the book of Hosea. Hosea was a prophet and God told him to take a prostitute for a wife. Hosea obeyed and married Gomer who was a prostitute and he loved her deeply. But Gomer could not accept his love and she left him and went back to her prostitution. Hosea went and found her and brought her home but she left him again to go back to her old life.

   c. The life of Hosea was a picture of Israel and God. God has taken Israel and us, because we are grafted into Israel, as His bride but we have turned away back to our prostitution because we cannot accept His love. Gomer is a perfect example of being envious of ourselves. She was envious of herself because she could not possibly think that Hosea could truly love her as she was. When we are envious of ourselves we are unable to accept the good in our lives and would rather wallow in a pig sty.

   d. Romans 8:28 "And we know that all things work together for good to those who love God, to those who are the called according to His purpose." The way we act on the decision to not envy ourselves is to accept that God is a good God and that He will even use the bad things in our lives to bring about good consequences if we trust in Him and allow Him to do what He needs to do in us to take us out of the pig sty.

4. Make a conscious decision to not be glad when others experience pain and not to crave what they have and then act on that decision.

    a. We are not to be envious or covet what other people around us have. Hebrews 13:5 tells us; "Let your conduct be without covetousness; be content with such things as you have. For He Himself has said, "I will never leave you nor forsake you." We are to be content with what we have and not begrudge others what they have.

    b. We must also not rejoice when others are hurting but rejoice with those that rejoice and mourn with those that mourn. Romans 12:15 "Rejoice with those who rejoice, and weep with those who weep."

    c. Another way to not be envious of others is to bear one another's burdens. Galatians 6:1-2 "Brethren, if a man is overtaken in any trespass, you who are spiritual restore such a one in a spirit of gentleness, considering yourself lest you also be tempted. Bear one another's burdens, and so fulfill the law of Christ." Everyone has some sort of burden to bear and if we would help them to bear that burden then we would no longer be envious of them.

Loving By Faith Bible Study

Loving by Faith Journal

Week 5

Choose **ONE** of the steps of not being envious and discuss how you feel about that step, what God may have shown you regarding that step and how you will incorporate that step into your life.

1. Make a conscious choice to believe that God is not glad when we experience misfortune or pain or that He wants what we have and then act on that decision.

2. Make a conscious decision to not be glad when God experiences pain or to want what God has and then act on that decision.

3. Make a conscious decision to not be glad when we experience pain and to not despise the good things in our lives and then act on that decision.

4. Make a conscious decision to not be glad when others experience pain and not to crave what they have and then act on that decision.

Loving By Faith Bible Study

Week 6

– Love does not boast, it is not proud

I. If we are to love by faith, then we need to understand what love is.

   A. To understand what love is we must look at 1 Corinthians 13:4-8a "Love is patient, love is kind. It does not envy, it does not boast, it is not proud. It does not dishonor others, it is not self-seeking, it is not easily angered, and it keeps no record of wrongs. Love does not delight in evil but rejoices with the truth. It always protects, always trusts, always hopes, and always perseveres. Love never fails."

   B. Each week we will examine each aspect of love in these verses and apply the four-step process to each aspect.

II. This week we will look at boasting and pride. Love does not boast; it is not proud.

   A. What is the definition of boasting?

      1. *Kaúxēma* – boasting, focusing on the results of exulting/boasting. This boasting (exulting) is always positive when it is in the Lord, and always negative when based on self.

      2. *Kauxáomai* – properly, living with "head up high," i.e. boasting from a particular vantage point by having the right base of operation to deal successfully with a matter. *Kauxáomai* likely comes from the root, auχēn ("neck"), i.e. what holds the head up high (upright); figuratively, it refers to living with God-given confidence.

      3. Boasting is a statement in which you express too much pride in yourself or in something you have, have done, or are connected to in some way: a reason to be proud: something impressive that someone or something has or has done

   B. What is the definition of pride?

      1. *Hyperēphanía* – properly, excessive shining, i.e. self-exaltation (self-absorption) which carries its own self-destructive vanity. *Hyperēphanía* is used only in Mk 7:22.

2. *Hyperḗphanos* – properly, over-shine, trying to be more than what God directs, i.e. going beyond the faith He imparts.

C. So, in the context of 1 Corinthians 13:4, love does not exalt itself with its head held high; it is not self-absorbed or trying to be more than what God directs.

D. Now let's apply the four-step process to boasting and pride.

  1. Make a conscious choice to believe that God does not exalt Himself or is self-absorbed and act on that decision.

    a. Jesus said in Luke 14:11 "For whoever exalts himself will be humbled, and he who humbles himself will be exalted."

    b. Not only did Jesus say this but He put it into practice as well. He humbled Himself to the point of death by allowing Himself to die a criminal's death, so we could have a relationship with the Father.

    c. Because of His humbling Himself, God exalted Him by raising Him from the dead and seating Jesus at His right hand.

    d. Jesus sacrificed Himself for us! This shows us that He is not self-absorbed because someone who is self-absorbed and full of pride would NEVER lower himself to die a criminal's death for someone else.

    e. We must make a conscious choice to believe that this is true but how do we act on that decision? We act on that decision by worshiping Jesus and exalting Him in our lives.

    f. Luke 19:37-41 "Then, as He was now drawing near the descent of the Mount of Olives, the whole multitude of the disciples began to rejoice and praise God with a loud voice for all the mighty works they had seen, saying: "Blessed is the King who comes in the name of the Lord! Peace in heaven and glory in the highest!" And some of the Pharisees called to Him from the crowd, "Teacher, rebuke Your disciples." But He answered and said to them, "I tell you that if these should keep silent, the stones would immediately cry out." Now as He drew near, He saw the city and wept over it, saying, "If you had known, even you, especially in this your day, the things that make for your peace! But now they are hidden from your eyes."

g. Notice that Jesus said that if we don't worship Him then the rocks will worship Him. This may come across as prideful but look what he does immediately following that statement: He saw the city of Jerusalem and wept over it because they do not know what will bring them peace. This is not a man full of pride but full of compassion and love. We must believe that and then worship Him because of that belief.

2. This step will be a bit different than the pattern I have developed. Make a conscious choice to exalt God and to be absorbed in Him and act on that decision. Remember boasting is always a good thing when we are boasting in the Lord.

   a. 2 Corinthians 10:17 But, "Let the one who boasts boast in the Lord." (NIV)

   b. If we are to boast and take pride in something, then the only thing we are to boast about is what God has done in our lives.

   c. Jeremiah 9:23-24 "This is what the Lord says: "Let not the wise boast of their wisdom or the strong boast of their strength, or the rich boast of their riches, but let the one who boasts boast about this: that they have the understanding to know me, that I am the Lord, who exercises kindness, justice and righteousness on earth, for in these I delight," declares the Lord." (NIV)

   d. When we exalt God, and boast about His love and kindness to us then we are doing what pleases God.

3. Make a conscious decision to not exalt yourself with your head held high and to not be self-absorbed and then act on that decision.

   a. We live in a "me" generation. This "me" generation exalts themselves and strives to make themselves seem bigger and better than they really are. This "me" generation also refuses to humble themselves enough to admit their mistakes and take responsibility for those mistakes. These issues have also seeped into the Church.

   b. James 4:10 "Humble yourselves in the sight of the Lord, and He will lift you up." When we humble ourselves, God will raise us up in His time. So, what is humility?

    i.   *Tapeinophrosýnē* (a noun, derived from *tapeinós*, "low, humble" and *phrḗn*, "moderation as regulated by inner perspective") – properly, low; humility, "lowliness" of human pride (self-government); that quality of mindset of "having a humble opinion of oneself, i.e. a deep sense of one's (moral) littleness – i.e. lowliness of mind".

    ii.   In Scripture, *tapeinophrosýnē* ("lowliness, humility") is an inside-out virtue produced by comparing ourselves to the Lord (rather than to others). This brings behavior into alignment with this inner revelation to keep one from being self-exalting (self-determining, self-inflated). For the believer, *tapeinophrosýnē* ("humility") means living in complete dependence on the Lord, i.e. with no reliance on self (the flesh).

    iii.   Humility is the opposite of pride. Pride exalts itself, but humility lowers itself.

    c.   When we lower ourselves, and exalt Christ then in God's timing, He will raise us up. But if we exalt ourselves in pride then God will bring us down. Proverbs 16:18 "Pride goes before destruction, and a haughty spirit before a fall."

4. Make a conscious decision to not exalt other people above God and to not be overly absorbed in another person over God and then act on that decision.

    a.   In the Church, we tend to exalt Pastors and TV Evangelists above God. We want to place these ministers on pedestals and put all our hope and expectation on them, but they are only people and they will fail us. This boils down to idolatry. Exodus 20:3 "You shall have no other gods before Me."

    b.   God and His Scripture should ALWAYS be number 1 in your life. This means God should even come before your spouse or your children. A spouse and children will leave you, but God never will. A spouse may walk away or even die and children will grow up and leave the nest. If you exalt those people over God in your life, then when they are gone you are left alone and have nothing left to live for. But if you will exalt Jesus above everyone else He says in Hebrews 13:5 "Let your conduct be without covetousness; be content with such things as you have. For He Himself has said, "I will never leave you nor forsake you."

c. When we exalt other people over God we are putting our faith in the wrong place. People will fail us, but God never will. He is the ONLY person we should be lifting and exalting.

d. So how do we act on the decision to not exalt other people above God? With a Pastor, the way we do that is to test EVERYTHING they say by Scripture. Study the Scripture for yourself and if the Pastor's message does not agree with Scripture then ignore it and dismiss it. With a spouse or children that means we put our trust in God first then we trust our family. And the same holds true for a husband as does a Pastor. If what a husband says does not line up with Scripture, then his words should be over-ruled by Scripture.

Loving by Faith Journal

Week 6

Choose **ONE** of the steps of not being envious and discuss how you feel about that step, what God may have shown you regarding that step and how you will incorporate that step into your life.

1. Make a conscious choice to believe that God does not exalt Himself or is self-absorbed and act on that decision.

2. Make a conscious choice to exalt God and to be absorbed in Him and act on that decision.

3. Make a conscious decision to not exalt yourself with your head held high and to not be self-absorbed and then act on that decision.

4. Make a conscious decision to not exalt other people above God and to not be overly absorbed in another person over God and then act on that decision.

Week 7

– Love does not dishonor others

I. If we are to love by faith, then we need to understand what love is.

    A. To understand what love is we must look at 1 Corinthians 13:4-8a "Love is patient, love is kind. It does not envy, it does not boast, it is not proud. It does not dishonor others, it is not self-seeking, it is not easily angered, and it keeps no record of wrongs. Love does not delight in evil but rejoices with the truth. It always protects, always trusts, always hopes, and always perseveres. Love never fails."

    B. Each week we will examine each aspect of love in these verses and apply the four-step process to each aspect.

II. This week we are examining the fact that love does not dishonor.

    A. Love does not dishonor others. This is stated in the negative and it may be easier to understand if we turned it around and stated it in the positive. So, to say the same thing in a positive way it will read: Love honors others. What does it mean to honor? When we learn to honor someone, we will not dishonor them.

        1. HELPS Word-studies defines honor as *timé* – properly, perceived value; worth (literally, "price") especially as perceived honor – i.e. what has value in the eyes of the beholder; (figuratively) the value (weight, honor) willingly assigned to something. (My observation here: the spelling of this Greek word is the same as our English word "time" so maybe part of the definition of honor is to give your time to the person you are honoring.)

        2. Strong's Exhaustive Concordance: honor, price, some. From *tino*; a value, i.e. Money paid, or (concretely and collectively) valuables; by analogy, esteem (especially of the highest degree), or the dignity itself -- honour, precious, price, some.

        3. HELPS Word-studies: *dóksa* ("glory") corresponds to the OT word, *kabo* ("to be heavy"). Both terms convey God's infinite, intrinsic worth (substance, essence). [(*dóksa*) literally means "what evokes good opinion, i.e. that something has inherent, intrinsic worth" (J. Thayer).]

B. So, the definition of honor is see someone as valuable and worth the price that Jesus paid for them, to see them as precious, to have a good opinion of them. When we honor someone, we see them as having intrinsic worth.

C. Let's apply the four-step process to honoring.

1. Make a conscious choice to believe that God sees you as valuable and worth the price Jesus paid, to believe that God sees you as precious and then act on that belief.

   a. To act on this belief is to be convinced that God sees you as precious. This means we must build our faith in this area. Romans 10:17 "So then faith comes by hearing, and hearing by the word of God." We must hear the Word spoken to build our faith because that is how faith is built, through hearing.

   b. The best way to hear the Word is out of your own mouth. So, every day you should speak OUTLOUD John 3:16 "For God so loved the world that He gave His only begotten Son, that whoever believes in Him should not perish but have everlasting life." But instead of quoting it as it is in Scripture I want you to put you own name in the banks. "For God so loved _____ that He gave His only begotten Son, that when _____ believes in Him _____ should not perish but have everlasting life." So, if I was to speak this out-loud for myself I would say, "For God so loved **Amy** that He gave His only begotten Son, that when **Amy** believes in Him, **Amy** should not perish but have everlasting life." Speak this out-loud every day and soon you will feel your self-worth improving. You do not have to say it loudly. You can speak it under your breath just as long as your ears can hear it. The more you do this the more you will start to experience how much God truly loves you.

   c. When you first start this, it will feel strange and you may even feel stupid but DO NOT GIVE UP! Satan does not want you to truly realize how valuable God sees you, so he will make you feel stupid when you first start this but do it anyway. It does not have to be done where anyone else can hear you. This is for YOU not anyone else!

2. Make a conscious decision to see God as valuable and precious. That God Himself has intrinsic value in your life and then act on that belief.

   a. 1 Samuel 2:30 "Therefore the Lord God of Israel says: 'I said indeed that your house and the house of your father would walk before Me forever.' But now the Lord says: 'Far be it from Me; for those who honor Me I will honor, and those who despise Me shall be lightly esteemed."

   b. Psalm 29:2 "Ascribe to the LORD the glory due to His name; Worship the LORD in holy array."

   c. When we honor God, we worship Him. Worship is much more than just singing praise songs. Worship means you "lift up" the object of your worship; to make Him higher then yourself.

   d. We worship God in many ways; by obeying Him, by praising Him, and by communicating with Him. (See my definitions of worship in week 5)

3. Make a conscious choice to see yourself as valuable and precious; to choose to believe that the price Jesus paid for you was worth it, that you have intrinsic value and then to act on that belief.

   a. This may be the hardest part for some people because we know how messed up we are, and we know all the bad things we have ever done or thought so how can we possibly honor ourselves?

   b. As you consider how God honors you by seeing you as valuable then the next natural step will be to see yourself in the same way. This may take some time and practice, but it will happen.

   c. Reject thoughts like "I am an idiot" or "what is wrong with me". Yes, you can reject some thoughts. You can control your thoughts. Your thoughts do not control you. When those thoughts come into your brain you can reject them and say, "I am the righteousness of God in Christ" (2 Corinthians 5:21 "For He made Him who knew no sin to be sin for us, that we might become the righteousness of God in Him.")

   d. Purposely think thoughts like, "God honored me enough to sentence his own Son to death for me then I can honor myself". Then act on that belief by doing something that will lift yourself up. That will be different for everyone. Listen to uplifting music, keep a journal, take a bubble bath, or go for a walk in the country. Treat yourself with the same kind of honor you would want someone else to treat you with. Give yourself some time as well.

4. Make a conscious choice to see other people as valuable and precious and that the price Jesus paid for them was worth it, to choose to believe that they have intrinsic value and then to act on that belief.

   a. Prejudice and discrimination is the opposite of honor. Every person, no matter their color, culture, income level, height or weight or sexual orientation are the same in God's eyes. Jesus died for Osama Bin Laden in the same way He died for you.

   b. Another way to honor other people is to give them your time. Remember the first Greek word I gave for the definition of honor was timé. This is spelled just like our English word for time, so we should give our time to the people we honor. It is not just time either but attention; when we honor someone, we give them all our attention because we believe they are worth our attention. What or who we honor will be where we give our time and attention.

Amy Leigh Moore

Loving by Faith Journal

Week 7

Choose **ONE** of the steps of honor and discuss how you feel about that step, what God may have shown you regarding that step and how you will incorporate that step into your life.

1. Make a conscious choice to believe that God sees you as valuable and worth the price Jesus paid, to believe that God sees you as precious and then act on that belief.

2. Make a conscious decision to see God as valuable and precious. That God Himself has intrinsic value in your life and then act on that belief.

3. Make a conscious choice to see yourself as valuable and precious; to choose to believe that the price Jesus paid for you was worth it, that you have intrinsic value and then to act on that belief.

4. Make a conscious choice to see other people as valuable and precious and that the price Jesus paid for them was worth it, to choose to believe that they have intrinsic value and then to act on that belief.

Week 8

– Love is not self-seeking

I. If we are to love by faith, then we need to understand what love is.

   A. To understand what love is we must look at 1 Corinthians 13:4-8a "Love is patient, love is kind. It does not envy, it does not boast, it is not proud. It does not dishonor others, it is not self-seeking, it is not easily angered, and it keeps no record of wrongs. Love does not delight in evil but rejoices with the truth. It always protects, always trusts, always hopes, and always perseveres. Love never fails."

   B. Each week we will examine each aspect of love in these verses and apply the four-step process to each aspect.

II. This week we will be examining the fact that Love is not self-seeking. Another way to say this is that love is not selfish.

   A. The Greek word for selfish is *eritheía* ("mercenary self-seeking") of acting for one's own gain, regardless of the discord (strife) it causes. *Eritheía* ("selfish ambition") places self-interest ahead of what the Lord declares right, or what is good for others.

   B. The dictionary's definition of selfish is concerned excessively or exclusively with oneself: seeking or concentrating on one's own advantage, pleasure, or well-being without regard for others or arising from concern with one's own welfare or advantage in disregard of others a selfish act

   C. Notice that both definitions say that selfishness is caring about yourself without regard of how that affects other people or any other consequences. We need to care about ourselves; that is not wrong. When it becomes selfishness is when we care more for ourselves then we do other people or when we care more for ourselves without concern about the consequences of our actions.

   D. One thing I like about the Greek definition is that it adds the part about what the Lord declares is right. So, we are selfish when we put ourselves ahead of what God says is right. That puts a whole different light on selfishness.

E. An actual definition of selfishness is putting ourselves and our wants and desires ahead of what God says is right or ahead of the needs of other people with no regards for the consequences of our actions.

F. So, let's apply the four steps to not being selfish.

1. Make a conscious decision to believe that God does not put His own wants and desires ahead of what He says is right or ahead of the needs of others with no regards for the consequences and act on that decision.

    a. God chose to create us, so He could have someone to love. He did not have to create this world or us, but He did, so He could have someone to love. He also gave us free will, so we could choose whether we would love Him in return. Again, He did not have to give us free will, but he did because He did not want us to be robots. On top of that, God willingly gave up some of His Power so that we could have free will. God will NEVER overrule our free will.

    b. Because we have free will then we will mess up but when we mess up God is there to heal us. But we have to turn away from our sins before He will heal us. 1 John 1:9 "If we confess our sins, He is faithful and just to forgive us our sins and to cleanse us from all unrighteousness."

    c. God sent His Only Son to die a brutal death just so we would not have to suffer the consequences of our sin. For those of you who are parents, would you be willing to do that? John 3:16 "For God so loved the world that He gave His only begotten Son, that whoever believes in Him should not perish but have everlasting life. Romans 6:23 "For the wages of sin is death, but the gift of God *is* eternal life in Christ Jesus our Lord."

2. Make a conscious decision to not put your own wants and desires ahead of God with no regards for the consequences and act on that decision.

    a. Matthew 6:33 "But seek first the kingdom of God and His righteousness, and all these things shall be added to you." Most Christians only see the second part of this verse, "all these things shall be added to you" but that is not the focus of this verse. That is the focus of selfishness. The focus of this verse is to "SEEK FIRST the kingdom of

God and His righteousness". So how do we seek first the kingdom of God and His righteousness?

b. The Greek word for seek is *zēteō* – properly, to seek by inquiring; to investigate to reach a binding (terminal) resolution; to search, "getting to the bottom of a matter." This is talking about intense searching and not being willing to give up until you have your answer. This is how we are to seek after God.

c. By seeking after God in this way, we put Him ahead of our own wants and desires and we are truly loving God because we are not being selfish. Also notice that the way that 1 Corinthians 13 says selfish is SELF-SEEKING. It uses the same word as Matthew 6:33 uses to seek after God. When we are self-seeking we are seeking ourselves more than we seek God and we are not the answer for our problems. God is.

3. Make a conscious decision to not put your own wants and desires ahead of what God says is right or ahead of the needs of yourself with no regards for the consequences and act on that decision.

a. We need to take time for ourselves and take time to recharge our batteries. Even Jesus took time for Himself away from His disciples. Matthew 14:22-23 "Immediately Jesus made His disciples get into the boat and go before Him to the other side, while He sent the multitudes away. And when He had sent the multitudes away, He went up on the mountain by Himself to pray. Now when evening came, He was alone there."

b. He needed time alone to pray and recharge and we need to do the same thing. That is something that God says is right and something we need. If we did not take the time to recharge, then we will exhaust ourselves and be no good to anyone.

c. If we don't take that time, then we are not considering the long-term consequences of our actions and that is ultimately a very selfish act. Not taking time for ourselves can cause burnout.

d. Here is a very good description of burnout. "Recent research has found that burnout--and the related concept of "vital exhaustion"--increases the risk for cardiovascular disease as much as such well-known risk factors as body mass index, smoking and lipid levels. Specifically, burnout increases people's likelihood of developing myocardial infarction, ischemic heart disease, stroke, and sudden cardiac death. Studies also point to an increased likelihood of type II diabetes, male infertility, sleep disorders and musculoskeletal disorders among those with the extreme physical, mental and emotional fatigue."

4. Make a conscious decision to not put your own wants and desires ahead of what God says is right or ahead of the needs of others with no regards for the consequences and act on that decision.

    a. Matthew 20:26-28 "Yet it shall not be so among you; but whoever desires to become great among you, let him be your servant. And whoever desires to be first among you, let him be your slave—just as the Son of Man did not come to be served, but to serve, and to give His life a ransom for many."

    b. There are books upon books written about servant leadership, yet many leaders have not figured it out. This book is just another way of talking about servant leadership. A good servant leader must always put the needs of his/her people ahead of their own needs.

    c. The best type of leader to follow is a servant leader. A servant leader engenders great respect and loyalty from their people because they put their people's needs ahead of their own needs and they sacrifice for their people. When people see a leader do that they are much more willing to sacrifice their wants and desires in return.

    d. But this is not just for leaders, if we are truly going love other people then we need to put their well-being ahead of our own. This can be done in many ways; too many ways that can be mentioned in a short Bible study.

Loving by Faith Journal

Week 8

Choose **ONE** of the steps of not being selfish and discuss how you feel about that step, what God may have shown you regarding that step and how you will incorporate that step into your life.

1. Make a conscious decision to believe that God does not put His own wants and desires ahead of what He says is right or ahead of the needs of others with no regards for the consequences and act on that decision.

2. Make a conscious decision to not put your own wants and desires ahead of God with no regards for the consequences and act on that decision.

3. Make a conscious decision to not put your own wants and desires ahead of what God says is right or ahead of the needs of yourself with no regards for the consequences and act on that decision.

4. Make a conscious decision to not put your own wants and desires ahead of what God says is right or ahead of the needs of others with no regards for the consequences and act on that decision.

Week 9

– Love is not easily angered

I. If we are to love by faith, then we need to understand what love is.

   A. To understand what love is we must look at 1 Corinthians 13:4-8a "Love is patient, love is kind. It does not envy, it does not boast, it is not proud. It does not dishonor others, it is not self-seeking, it is not easily angered, and it keeps no record of wrongs. Love does not delight in evil but rejoices with the truth. It always protects, always trusts, always hopes, and always perseveres. Love never fails."

   B. Each week we will examine each aspect of love in these verses and apply the four-step process to each aspect.

II. This week we will be examining the fact that Love is not easily angered.

   A. So, what is anger?

   1. The Greek word for anger is *orgé* (from *orgáō*, "to teem, swelling up to constitutionally oppose") – properly, settled anger (opposition), i.e. rising up from an ongoing (fixed) opposition.

   2. *Orgé* ("settled anger") proceeds from an internal disposition which steadfastly opposes someone, or something based on extended personal exposure, i.e. solidifying what the beholder considers wrong (unjust, evil).

   3. "*Orgē* comes from the verb *oragō* meaning, 'to teem, to swell'; and thus implies that it is not a sudden outburst, but rather (referring to God's) fixed, controlled, passionate feeling against sin. . . a settled indignation

   4. This implies that anger is much more then losing one's temper. This is the type of anger that simmers under the surface for a long time.

   5. Ephesians 4:26 "Be angry, and do not sin"; do not let the sun go down on your wrath,"

   6. We can get angry and lose our temper without sinning. Jesus did it when He overturned the tables in the Temple. So, how can we be angry and not sin? We do this by not allowing that anger to simmer under the surface and

dwelling on what makes us angry. When we let the anger simmer, it can destroy our lives and that kind of anger is what is sin.

7. So, the definition of anger is a feeling of passionate indignation that we allow to stew under the surface and that we allow to color how we see the world around us.

B. Let's apply anger to the four-step process.

1. Make a conscious decision to believe that God does not easily get angry with us or harbor a feeling of passionate indignation that He allows to stew under the surface and that He allows to color how He views us.

   a. God does get angry with us. In Genesis 18, when 2 angels came to visit Abraham, they told Abraham that God was planning to destroy Sodom and Gomorrah because of their great sin and Abraham bargained with Him and received a promise from God that if He could find 10 righteous people in those places that He would not destroy those cities. He did not find 10 righteous people, so Sodom and Gomorrah were destroyed. This shows that even though God was angry enough to destroy two cities because of their unrighteousness, God was willing to turn away from that anger for the sake of 10 righteous people.

   b. The story of Jonah and Nineveh is another story of God turning away from His anger against people if they will repent. Jonah was sent to Nineveh to warn them that God was angry with them and that He was about to destroy their city and Jonah refused because he knew God was a God of mercy. Consequently, God caused a whale to swallow him and when Jonah was finally free from the whale, he obeyed God and went to Nineveh. The people of Nineveh repented, and God did not destroy them.

   c. God does get angry with us, but it takes a long time for Him to get angry and He is quick to turn from that anger when we repent of our sins and turn back to Him. Numbers 14:18 (NIV) 'The Lord is slow to anger, abounding in love and forgiving sin and rebellion. Yet he does not leave the guilty unpunished; he punishes the children for the sin of the parents to the third and fourth generation.' Nehemiah 9:17 (NIV) "They refused to listen and failed to remember the miracles you performed among them. They became stiff-necked and in their rebellion appointed a leader in order to return to their slavery. But you are a forgiving God, gracious and compassionate, slow to anger and abounding in love. Therefore, you did not desert them' Psalm 103:8 (NIV) "The Lord is compassionate and gracious, slow to anger, abounding in love."

2. Make a conscious decision to not easily get angry or harbor a feeling of passionate indignation toward God that you allow to stew under the surface and that you allow to color how you view God.

   a. When I was growing up, I was taught that it was wrong to get angry with God. I no longer believe that. There are times we are going to get angry with God because we do not fully understand what is happening or why it is happening.

   b. David got angry with God. "How long, O LORD? Will you forget me forever? How long will you hide your face from me? How long must I wrestle with my thoughts and every day have sorrow in my heart? How long will my enemy triumph over me? Look on me and answer, O LORD my God. Give light to my eyes, or I will sleep in death; my enemy will say, "I have overcome him," and my foes will rejoice when I fall. But I trust in your unfailing love; my heart rejoices in your salvation. I will sing to the LORD, for he has been good to me." (Psalm 13:1-6)

   c. "O Lord, how long will you look on? Rescue my life from their ravages, my precious life from these lions. I will give you thanks in the great assembly; among throngs of people I will praise you." (Psalm 35:17-18)

   d. "I say to God my Rock, "Why have you forgotten me? Why must I go about mourning, oppressed by the enemy?" My bones suffer mortal agony as my foes taunt me, saying to me all day long, "Where is your God?" Why are you downcast, O my soul? Why so disturbed within me? Put your hope in God, for I will yet praise him, my Savior and my God." (Psalm 42:9-11)

   e. In each instance, David started out angry but ended up praising God. We can do both. We can be angry because we do not understand what God is doing but in the end, we must decide whether or not to trust God

Loving By Faith Bible Study

or to walk away from Him. David decided to trust God. What will your choice be?

3. Make a conscious decision to not easily get angry or harbor a feeling of passionate indignation toward yourself that you allow to stew under the surface and that you allow to color how you view yourself.

   a. Romans 7:15 "For what I am doing, I do not understand. For what I will to do, that I do not practice; but what I hate, that I do."

   b. Have you ever done something you know is wrong and you know you did not want to do it but did it anyway? Paul had the same problem. How did he deal with it? Did he get angry with himself? No, he didn't.

   c. Instead of getting angry with himself, Paul just got closer to Jesus. Romans 7:22 "For I delight in the law of God according to the inward man."

   d. Romans 7:24-25 "O wretched man that I am! Who will deliver me from this body of death? I thank God—through Jesus Christ our Lord!" Paul acknowledged that he had a problem and instead of getting angry at himself about it, He just turned to Jesus. Paul loved himself enough to see himself honestly and admit his weakness. But instead of beating himself up over it, he turned to the only solution he knew; Jesus.

   e. That is how we should deal with our own shortcomings, as well. No one is perfect, so instead of getting angry with ourselves because of our shortcomings, we should turn more to Jesus to let Him make those shortcomings better.

4. Make a conscious decision to not easily get angry or harbor a feeling of passionate indignation toward other people that you allow to stew under the surface and that you allow to color how you view other people.

   a. Ephesians 4:26 "Be angry, and do not sin": do not let the sun go down on your wrath" Proverbs 15:1 "A soft answer turns away wrath, But, a harsh word stirs up anger." James 1:19-20 "So then, my beloved brethren, let every man be swift to hear, slow to speak, slow to wrath; for the wrath of man does not produce the righteousness of God."

b. There are a lot more verses on anger, but these are enough for our purposes. We can lose our temper, just as God does. We are made in His image, after all. But we should be slow to get angry just as He is, and we should be quick to turn away from that anger.

c. I have dealt with the elderly in my work and the elderly can sometimes be very difficult to deal with. Many of them have lost the concept of time management and their minds wander and it is sometimes hard to keep them on the subject at hand. I could get angry with them, but that anger will not accomplish anything. It will only cause them to be angry back at me and I could be disciplined by my boss. Instead of anger, I take a deep breath and become even sweeter to them. This usually calms the situation down.

d. Sometimes we don't have the time to truly listen to people but if we would take the time to listen instead of getting angry, this would alleviate much of the tensions in any situation.

e. So, when we get angry with other people, make a conscious effort to be nicer to them and make a conscious effort to listen more to them. If we would do that, then our anger will usually disappear.

Loving by Faith Journal

Week 9

Choose **ONE** of the steps of not being easily angered and discuss how you feel about that step, what God may have shown you regarding that step and how you will incorporate that step into your life.

1. Make a conscious decision to believe that God does not easily get angry with us or harbor a feeling of passionate indignation that He allows to stew under the surface and that He allows to color how He views us.

2. Make a conscious decision to not easily get angry or harbor a feeling of passionate indignation toward God that you allow to stew under the surface and that you allow to color how you view God.

3. Make a conscious decision to not easily get angry or harbor a feeling of passionate indignation toward yourself that you allow to stew under the surface and that you allow to color how you view yourself.

4. Make a conscious decision to not easily get angry or harbor a feeling of passionate indignation toward other people that you allow to stew under the surface and that you allow to color how you view other people.

Loving By Faith Bible Study

Week 10

– Love keeps no records of wrongs

I. If we are to love by faith, then we need to understand what love is.

　A. To understand what love is we must look at 1 Corinthians 13:4-8a "Love is patient, love is kind. It does not envy, it does not boast, it is not proud. It does not dishonor others, it is not self-seeking, it is not easily angered, and it keeps no record of wrongs. Love does not delight in evil but rejoices with the truth. It always protects, always trusts, always hopes, and always perseveres. Love never fails."

　B. Each week we will examine each aspect of love in these verses and apply the four-step process to each aspect.

II. This week we will examine the fact that Love does not keep any record of wrongs.

　A. The Greek word and meaning for "keep" is *tēréō* (from *tēros*, "a guard") – properly, maintain (preserve); (figuratively) *spiritually guard* (watch), *keep intact*.

　B. So, when we keep a record of the wrongs done to us, we are essentially guarding over those wrongs and keeping them intact. We dwell on them and let them control our thinking. We rehearse the wrong repeatedly in our mind. The wrong gnaws at us and we allow it to influence our thinking. We hold a grudge.

　C. How do we not hold a grudge? We forgive. What is forgiveness? The Greek word for forgiveness is *xarízomai* (from *xáris*, "grace, extending *favor*") – properly, to *extend favor* ("*grace*"), *freely give favor* to grant *forgiveness* (*pardon*). So, when we forgive we pardon or freely give favor to those that have hurt us.

　D. Then the definition of not keeping any record of wrongs is to forgive and not hold a grudge. Love forgives and does not hold grudges.

　E. Let's apply the fact that Love forgives and does not hold a grudge to the four-step process.

　　1. Make a conscious decision to believe that God forgives you and does not hold a grudge against you and then act on that decision.

a. 1 John 1:9 "If we confess our sins, He is faithful and just to forgive us our sins and to cleanse us from all unrighteousness." God is faithful to forgive us but there is a prerequisite for that forgiveness. We must confess those sins to God, not necessarily to other people.

b. Isaiah 43:25 "I, even I, am He who blots out your transgressions for My own sake; And I will not remember your sins." Hebrews 8:12 "For I will be merciful to their unrighteousness, and their sins and their lawless deeds I will remember no more."

c. God makes a conscious choice to not remember our sins once we have confessed and repented of those sins. Our action that we believe that is to confess and repent of our sins.

2. Make a conscious decision to forgive God and not hold a grudge against Him and then act on that decision.

a. Isaiah 55:8 "For My thoughts are not your thoughts, nor are your ways My ways," says the Lord." We do not always understand why bad things happen. We ask why God did not prevent bad things from happening. But God thinks very differently than we do. When something bad happens, we may want to blame God for it.

b. Psalm 18:30 "As for God, His way is perfect; The word of the Lord is proven; He is a shield to all who trust in Him." God is perfect and does not make mistakes but our understanding of His Ways is incomplete, so we may blame God when bad things happen.

c. Matthew 5:45 "that you may be sons of your Father in heaven; for He makes His sun rise on the evil and on the good, and sends rain on the just and on the unjust." When rain comes, we can either blame God and get angry with God or trust Him and believe that He knows best even if we don't understand.

d. For some people that process can start by forgiving God for a perceived hurt. God does not cause the hurt but there are times that we think He does because have an incomplete understanding of His ways. So, the first step for these people is to forgive God, let go of the anger and not hold a grudge toward God.

3. Make a conscious decision to forgive yourself and not hold a grudge against yourself and then act on that decision.

   a. Hebrews 9:14 "how much more shall the blood of Christ, who through the eternal Spirit offered Himself without spot to God, cleanse your conscience from dead works to serve the living God?" Jesus died a horrific death so that your sins could be forgiven and we could have a clean conscious.

   b. Colossians 3:13 "bearing with one another, and forgiving one another, if anyone has a complaint against another; even as Christ forgave you, so you also must do." The Greek word for "one another" is allélón: of one another. It is a genitive plural from allos reduplicated; one another -- each other, mutual, one another, (the other), (them-, your-) selves, (selves) together. Notice that yourself is included in this meaning. So, we also need to forgive ourselves just as we forgive other people.

   c. When we make a conscious decision to forgive ourselves and not hold a grudge against ourselves then we are putting into practice what Jesus died a horrible death to give us. If we can't forgive ourselves then how can we forgive other people?

4. Make a conscious decision to forgive others and to not hold a grudge against them and then act on that decision.

   a. Mark 11:25 "And whenever you stand praying, if you have anything against anyone, forgive him, that your Father in heaven may also forgive you your trespasses." Forgiveness is an instantaneous choice we can make at any time. It is not a process. A process takes time so if forgiveness was a process then God would be unjust in telling us to forgive as we stand praying. Forgiveness is a choice; healing is the process.

   b. Notice that also that God commands us to forgive other people and if we won't forgive then we cannot expect to be forgiven of our own sins. That is a scary proposition. I have not always done the right thing and the thought that I may not be forgiven of my mistakes scares me. So, I quickly forgive because I want to be forgiven quickly.

c. Leviticus 19:18 "You shall not take vengeance, nor bear any grudge against the children of your people, but you shall love your neighbor as yourself: I am the Lord." God tells us directly to not hold a grudge against other people in this verse. Holding a grudge and unforgiveness are as much sins as stealing or lying.

d. So, how do we forgive and not hold a grudge against those who have hurt us? We consciously choose to forgive and not hold a grudge, even if we don't feel like it. The miracle is if we will continually make those choices then God will change our feelings to match up with our choices. Does it happen immediately? Most often, no. But it will happen!

Loving By Faith Bible Study

Loving by Faith Journal

Week 10

Choose **ONE** of the steps of forgiving and not holding a grudge and discuss how you feel about that step, what God may have shown you regarding that step and how you will incorporate that step into your life.

1. Make a conscious decision to believe that God forgives you and does not hold a grudge against you and then act on that decision.

2. Make a conscious decision to forgive God and not hold a grudge against Him and then act on that decision.

3. Make a conscious decision to forgive yourself and not hold a grudge against yourself and then act on that decision.

4. Make a conscious decision to forgive others and to not hold a grudge against them and then act on that decision.

Loving By Faith Bible Study

Week 11

– Love does not delight in evil but rejoices in the Truth

I. If we are to love by faith, then we need to understand what love is.

   A. To understand what love is we must look at 1 Corinthians 13:4-8a "Love is patient, love is kind. It does not envy, it does not boast, it is not proud. It does not dishonor others, it is not self-seeking, it is not easily angered, and it keeps no record of wrongs. Love does not delight in evil but rejoices with the truth. It always protects, always trusts, always hopes, and always perseveres. Love never fails."

   B. Each week we will examine each aspect of love in these verses and apply the four-step process to each aspect.

II. This week we will examine the fact that Love does not delight in evil but rejoices with the truth.

   A. The Greek word for evil is **ponērós** – properly, *pain-ridden*, emphasizing the inevitable agonies (misery) that always go with *evil*. Other meanings include

   1. full of labors, annoyances, hardships;
   2. pressed and harassed by labors;
   3. bringing toils, annoyances, perils:
   4. causing pain and trouble
   5. bad, of a bad nature or condition;
   6. evil, wicked, bad, etc.

   B. The Greek word for truth is **alḗtheia** (from **alēthḗs**, "true to fact") – properly, truth (true to fact), reality. This does not give us much information because it is a circular definition, so I will turn to the Scripture for our definition of truth.

   C. John 14:6 "Jesus said to him, "I am the way, the truth, and the life. No one comes to the Father except through Me." Jesus is the Truth and He is the One that will set people free. John 8:32 "And you shall know the truth, and the truth shall make you free."

D. So, Love does not delight in things that that bring pain, agony, annoyances, hardships, or trouble but rejoices when we start to see Jesus in people and people become freed from the bondage that Satan and sin creates.

E. Let's apply this definition to the four-step process.

   1. Make a conscious decision to believe that God does not delight in things that bring pain, agony, annoyances, hardships, or trouble but rejoices when He starts to see Jesus in people and people become freed from the bondage that Satan and sin creates and then act on that decision.

      a. The shortest verse in Scripture is John 11:35 "Jesus wept." Jesus wept when He heard that his friend Lazarus had died, and He weeps when we weep.

      b. John 15:26 King James Version (KJV) "But when the Comforter is come, whom I will send unto you from the Father, even the Spirit of truth, which proceedeth from the Father, he shall testify of me" The fact that God has sent us a comforter in the Holy Spirit proves that He feels our pain. If He did not feel our pain, then He would not have sent us a Comforter.

      c. When my husband died, I felt more comforted by God then I have ever felt in my life. I felt a bubble of peace around me for months after my husband's death. I knew that I knew that God felt my deep pain and was right there to help me deal with it.

   2. Make a conscious decision to not delight in things that bring pain, agony, annoyances, hardships, or trouble to God but rejoice when we start to see Jesus in Scripture and act on that decision.

      a. God does experience pain. In Genesis, we see this verse. Genesis 6:5-6 New International Version (NIV) "The Lord saw how great the wickedness of the human race had become on the earth, and that every inclination of the thoughts of the human heart was only evil all the time. 6 The Lord regretted that he had made human beings on the earth, and his heart was deeply troubled." God felt pain when He saw how wicked men had become and He was also grieved by what He had to do to

b. Because God is a God of both Love and justice, He sent His Son to pay for our sins for us. Jesus suffered terribly during his crucifixion. If you have ever seen Mel Gibson's "Passion of the Christ" then you have seen an accurate portrayal of the pain Jesus endured. I could only watch that movie once. It was too graphic and had me weeping and begging them to stop hurting Him. But Jesus did that willingly because He loved us and because He knew that justice had to be served for our sin. We can delight in what Jesus did when He rose again, but we should never rejoice in His pain. Jesus cried out in agony in Matthew 27:46 "And about the ninth hour Jesus cried out with a loud voice, saying, "Eli, Eli, lama sabachthani?" that is, "My God, My God, why have You forsaken Me?"

c. Every time I think about what Jesus did for me, I want to weep. The pain He endured for me was unthinkable, but He did it because He loved me enough to pay my penalty for my sin for me. So now I can rejoice when He rose from the dead and finished everything for me as well. John 19:30 "So when Jesus had received the sour wine, He said, "It is finished!" And bowing His head, He gave up His spirit." He finished everything we need to live successful Godly lives when He died for us. We can rejoice in that.

3. Make a conscious decision to not delight in things that bring pain, agony, annoyances, hardships, or trouble to yourself but rejoice when you start to see Jesus in yourself and you become freed from the bondage that Satan and sin creates and then act on that decision.

a. Some people are not happy unless they are miserable. They delight in trouble. I cannot even imagine that, but it must be true because they live in trouble and heartache constantly and don't ever seem to want to get out of it.

b. Even when many of them are presented with a way out the return to their old ways. Proverbs 26:11 "As a dog returns to his own vomit, So, a fool repeats his folly."

c. This is a major sign that they do not love themselves. They do not feel they are worth anything better, so they stay in the pain and agony of their pain. They do not feel worthy of freedom or may not be willing to do the work necessary to get free, so they stay in the mess and rejoice in the mess. But God wants us to be free and rejoice in the freedom not the bondage!

4. Make a conscious decision to not delight in things that bring pain, agony, annoyances, hardships, or trouble to other people but rejoice when we start to see Jesus in people and people become freed from the bondage that Satan and sin creates and then act on that decision.

a. Romans 12:15 "Rejoice with those who rejoice, and weep with those who weep." We are to rejoice with people in their success and weep with those who are in the pain.

b. Galatians 6:2 "Bear one another's burdens, and so fulfill the law of Christ." When people are in pain, we should be right there beside them, helping them to carry that burden while at the same time helping them to get out of the pain. When they finally get past the pain then we can rejoice with them.

Loving By Faith Bible Study

Loving by Faith Journal

Week 11

Choose **ONE** of the steps of not delighting in things that that bring pain, agony, annoyances, hardships, or trouble but rejoices when we start to see Jesus in people and people become freed from the bondage that Satan and sin creates and discuss how you feel about that step, what God may have shown you regarding that step and how you will incorporate that step into your life.

1. Make a conscious decision to believe that God does not delight in things that bring pain, agony, annoyances, hardships, or trouble but rejoices when He starts to see Jesus in people and people become freed from the bondage that Satan and sin creates and then act on that decision.

2. Make a conscious decision to not delight in things that bring pain, agony, annoyances, hardships, or trouble to God but rejoice when we start to see Jesus in Scripture and act on that decision.

3. Make a conscious decision to not delight in things that bring pain, agony, annoyances, hardships, or trouble to yourself but rejoice when you start to see Jesus in yourself and you become freed from the bondage that Satan and sin creates and then act on that decision.

4. Make a conscious decision to not delight in things that bring pain, agony, annoyances, hardships, or trouble to other people but rejoice when we start to see Jesus in people and people become freed from the bondage that Satan and sin creates and then act on that decision.

Loving By Faith Bible Study

Week 12

– Love always protects

I. If we are to love by faith, then we need to understand what love is.

   A. To understand what love is we must look at 1 Corinthians 13:4-8a "Love is patient, love is kind. It does not envy, it does not boast, it is not proud. It does not dishonor others, it is not self-seeking, it is not easily angered, and it keeps no record of wrongs. Love does not delight in evil but rejoices with the truth. It always protects, always trusts, always hopes, and always perseveres. Love never fails."

   B. Each week we will examine each aspect of love in these verses and apply the four-step process to each aspect.

II. This week we will look at the fact that Love always protects.

   A. *Phylássō* – properly, preserve by "having an eye on", referring to the uninterrupted vigilance shepherds show in keeping their flocks

   B. *Phylássō* - ("keep watch over, keep secure") emphasizes the needed vigilance to keep what is entrusted. Thus (*phylássō*) is often used in the NT in the Greek middle voice meaning, "Personally be on guard against," stressing the constant, personal interest involved with the guarding.

   C. Other definitions include: to guard, watch, abstain, guard, guarded, guarding, guards, keep, keeping, keeps, kept, kept under guard, maintain, observe, preserved, protect, watching.

   D. Another word for protect is *tēréō* (from *tēros*, "a guard") – properly, maintain (preserve); (figuratively) spiritually guard (watch), keep intact.

   E. Other definitions of *tēréō* include: to watch over, to guard, continue, guard, guards, heed, heeds, held in custody, keep, keep watch over, keeping, keeping guard over, keeps, kept, kept in custody, observe, preserve, preserved, reserved, watching over.

   F. So, the definition of protecting is to guard over or to keep, maintain or watch over. Love always guards over, keeps, maintains, and watches over the object of that love.

G. Let's apply protection to the four-step process.

1. Make a conscious decision to believe that God guards over, keeps, maintains, and watches over you and act on that decision.

    a. Psalm 121:7-8 New International Version (NIV) "The Lord will keep you from all harm—he will watch over your life; the Lord will watch over your coming and going both now and forevermore."

    b. Psalm 91:1-4 "He who dwells in the secret place of the Most High Shall abide under the shadow of the Almighty. I will say of the Lord, "He is my refuge and my fortress; My God, in Him I will trust." Surely, He shall deliver you from the snare of the fowler And from the perilous pestilence. He shall cover you with His feathers, And under His wings you shall take refuge; His truth shall be your shield and buckler."

    c. Notice that in Psalms 91 we must dwell in the secret place to receive this protection. We have a choice to make. If we will dwell in that secret place, then God will protect us. Our willingness to dwell in that secret place is our action that tells God we truly believe that He will protect us.

2. Make a conscious decision to guard over, keep, maintain, and watch over God and His Word and act on that decision.

    a. John 15:9-10 "As the Father loved Me, I also have loved you; abide in My love. If you keep My commandments, you will abide in My love, just as I have kept My Father's commandments and abide in His love."

    b. Psalm 119:1-3 "Blessed are the undefiled in the way, Who walk in the law of the Lord! Blessed are those who keep His testimonies, Who seek Him with the whole heart! They also do no iniquity; they walk in His ways."

    c. When we keep or protect God's Word that proves our love for Him. We are also blessed when we keep His Word. So, how do we keep God's Word. We read the Bible daily and meditate on the Scripture. To meditate on it means that we turn it over and over in our minds and consider it from many different perspectives. This Bible study is the perfect example of keeping God's Word.

3. Make a conscious decision to guard over, keep, maintain, and watch over yourself and act on that decision.

   a. 1 John 5:18 "We know that whoever is born of God does not sin; but he who has been born of God keeps himself, and the wicked one does not touch him."

   b. Proverbs 4:23 "Keep your heart with all diligence, For out of it spring the issues of life."

   c. We need to keep ourselves and our hearts from the attacks of Satan. This means we need use wisdom and discernment to know what is truth and what is a lie. One way to do this is to prove everything by Scripture. To do this we need to know what Scripture says; not what the Pastor says about Scripture.

4. Make a conscious decision to guard over, keep, maintain, and watch over other people and act on that decision.

   a. Psalm 82:3-4 "Defend the poor and fatherless; Do justice to the afflicted and needy. Deliver the poor and needy; Free them from the hand of the wicked."

   b. Proverbs 24:11 "Deliver those who are drawn toward death, And hold back those stumbling to the slaughter."

   c. When we love people, we want to protect them. That is a God-given instinct. But many people do not understand this. When I was a child, my step-father sexually molested my two sisters and I and my mother found out about it. But she was taught that protecting her marriage was more important than protecting her children, so she stayed in her marriage. But if you will notice these verses never say to protect a situation or circumstance. It says we are to protect the needy and the poor and those who are drawn toward death. People are to be protected not situations or circumstances.

Loving by Faith Journal

Week 12

Choose **ONE** of the steps of Love guarding over, keeping, maintaining, and watching over the object of that Love and discuss how you feel about that step, what God may have shown you regarding that step and how you will incorporate that step into your life.

1. Make a conscious decision to believe that God guards over, keeps, maintains, and watches over you and act on that decision.

2. Make a conscious decision to guard over, keep, maintain, and watch over God and His Word and act on that decision.

3. Make a conscious decision to guard over, keep, maintain, and watch over yourself and act on that decision.

4. Make a conscious decision to guard over, keep, maintain, and watch over other people and act on that decision.

Week 13

– Love always trusts

I. If we are to love by faith, then we need to understand what love is.

   A. To understand what love is we must look at 1 Corinthians 13:4-8a "Love is patient, love is kind. It does not envy, it does not boast, it is not proud. It does not dishonor others, it is not self-seeking, it is not easily angered, and it keeps no record of wrongs. Love does not delight in evil but rejoices with the truth. It always protects, always trusts, always hopes, and always perseveres. Love never fails."

   B. Each week we will examine each aspect of love in these verses and apply the four-step process to each aspect.

II. This week we will look at the fact that Love always trusts.

   A. The Greek word for trust is *peithō* (the root *pístis*, "faith") – to persuade; (passive) be persuaded of what is trustworthy.

   B. Notice that we must be persuaded to trust. Trust is not something that is freely given. Trust must be earned through persuasion and action. But once that trust is earned than love will always trust.

   C. Other definitions of *peithō* include: to persuade, to have confidence, assure, confident, convinced, followed, have confidence, having confidence, listen, obey, obeying, persuade, persuaded, persuading, put...trust, put confidence, put...confidence, relied, seeking the favor, sure, took...advice, trust, trusted, trusting, trusts, urging, win...over, won over.

   D. So, Love always allows itself to be persuaded to put our confidence in and rely on the object of that love.

   E. Let's apply always trusting to the four-step process.

   1. Make a conscious decision to allow God to persuade you that He is trustworthy and then act on that decision.

      a. Malachi 3:10 "Bring all the tithes into the storehouse, that there may be food in My house, And try Me now in this," Says the Lord of hosts, "If I will not open for you the windows of heaven And pour out for you such blessing That there will not be room enough to receive it."

b. There are other verses that tell us we are not to test the Lord, but I believe the permissibility of testing God has to do with our motives. If our motive for testing God is to find out whether we can trust Him to do what He says, then I think it is something God does not have a problem with. But if our motive is to disprove Him or to mock Him then we should not be testing Him. God is giving us a dare in Malachi. Will we dare to do what He tells us to do and test to see if He will do His part once we do our part? There are many other verses that do something similar.

c. John 15:7 "If you abide in Me, and My words abide in you, you will ask what you desire, and it shall be done for you." Notice the prerequisite here; we are to abide in Jesus and His Word must abide in us before we can ask what we want, and it will be done for us. Jesus is almost giving us a dare here. Abide in me and then ask what you want and see if I won't do it for you? This verse is what got me to ORU.

2. Make a conscious decision to believe that God will give you opportunities to persuade Him that you are trustworthy and act on that decision.

a. Matthew 25:14-30 "For the kingdom of heaven is like a man traveling to a far country, who called his own servants and delivered his goods to them. And to one he gave five talents, to another two, and to another one, to each according to his own ability; and immediately he went on a journey. Then he who had received the five talents went and traded with them, and made another five talents. And likewise, he who had received two gained two more also. But he who had received one went and dug in the ground, and hid his lord's money. After a long time, the lord of those servants came and settled accounts with them. "So, he who had received five talents came and brought five other talents, saying, 'Lord, you delivered to me five talents; look, I have gained five more talents besides them.' His lord said to him, 'Well done, good and faithful servant; you were faithful over a few things, I will make you ruler over many things. Enter into the joy of your lord.' He also who had received two talents came and said, 'Lord, you delivered to me two talents; look, I have gained two more talents besides them.' His lord said to him, 'Well done, good and faithful servant; you have been faithful over a few things, I will make you ruler over many things. Enter into the joy of your lord.' "Then he who had received the one talent came and said, 'Lord, I knew you to be a hard man, reaping where you have not sown, and gathering where you have not scattered seed. And I was afraid, and went and hid your talent in the ground. Look, there you have what is yours.' "But his lord answered and said to him, 'You wicked and lazy servant, you knew that I reap where I have not sown, and gather where I have not scattered seed. So, you ought to have deposited my money with the bankers, and at my coming I would have received back my own with interest. Therefore, take the talent from him, and give it to him who has ten talents. 'For to everyone who has, more will be given, and he will have abundance; but from him who does not have, even what he has will be taken away. 30 And cast the unprofitable servant into the outer darkness. There will be weeping and gnashing of teeth.'

    b.   Just as this lord did for his servants, God will give us opportunities to use what He has given us for His benefit. As we become faithful in small things, we prove our trustworthiness to God and then He will give us bigger things.

3.   Make a conscious decision to persuade yourself that you are trustworthy (only if your thoughts and actions line up with Scripture) and then act on that decision.

    a.   The Bible never says to trust in yourself. It says in Proverbs 3:5-6 "Trust in the Lord with all your heart, and lean not on your own understanding; In all your ways acknowledge Him, And He shall direct your paths."

    b.   I fully believe that we are to study the Scriptures for ourselves and not rely on a Pastor to interpret Scripture for us. 2 Timothy 2:15 "Be diligent to present yourself approved to God, a worker who does not need to be ashamed, rightly dividing the word of truth."

c. John 14:26 "But the Helper, the Holy Spirit, whom the Father will send in My name, He will teach you all things, and bring to your remembrance all things that I said to you." When we study the Scripture for ourselves, we allow the Holy Spirit to teach us things that no one else may have seen.

d. These revelations from the Holy Spirit are what we must trust in even if they go against traditional Church doctrine. We need to be so persuaded to trust in these revelations that not one person could make us unbelieve those revelations.

e. But to be able to trust in our revelations from the Holy Spirit, we must first know what the Scripture says for ourselves AND know how to hear from the Holy Spirit. Learning to hear the Holy Spirit takes time and practice. We must also remember that the Holy Spirit will NEVER tell us something that goes against the written Word. So, if you think a revelation is from the Holy Spirit then ask Him to show it to you in Scripture. If the revelation cannot be backed up by the written Word, then it is not the Holy Spirit.

f. This is where this book has come from. The Holy Spirit has taught me these things and not one person could make me believe otherwise. I trust in the interpretation of Scripture the Holy Spirit has revealed to me over and above what people say. Now does that mean I have everything right? Not at all! I could be wrong but for someone to show me I am wrong they would need to use Scripture to do it.

g. The reason I am so adamant about believing the interpretation the Holy Spirit has taught me is because I saw my mother believe the interpretation of Scripture by the Pastor and she stayed in an abusive marriage because of it. She told me that she had been feeling like God was telling her to leave her husband because he was abusing her daughters. But the Pastor told her that her marriage should be preserved using 1 Peter 3:1-2, so she should stay and submit and believe that through that submission, God would change her husband. She had no confidence in her own ability to hear from the Holy Spirit, so she believed the Pastor's interpretation of Scripture over what she felt God was telling her. If a person's, even a Pastor's, interpretation of Scripture causes a person to be abused in any way then that interpretation is wrong. God does not want His people to be abused.

4. Make a conscious decision to allow other people to persuade you that they are trustworthy and then act on that decision.

   a. John 2:23-25 New International Version (NIV) "Now while he was in Jerusalem at the Passover Festival, many people saw the signs he was performing and believed in his name. But Jesus would not entrust himself to them, for he knew all people. He did not need any testimony about mankind, for he knew what was in each person." Who was it that Jesus did not trust? Was it the Pharisees? The Disciples? Or just people in general? Look at the context of this verse. Jesus was at the Passover Festival and in the passage just before this one (John 2:13-22), Jesus turned over the money changer's tables for cheating the people, which angered the Priests. So, Jesus knew better than to trust Himself with the people at the Passover Festival. But that does not mean that He did not trust anyone.

   b. John 13:23 "Now there was leaning on Jesus' bosom one of His disciples, whom Jesus loved." Most scholars believe that John was describing himself in this verse. John is known as the disciple of love.

   c. John proved himself to be trustworthy to Jesus, so he had an eyewitness account of things the other disciples did not record. The book of John has more unique stories of Jesus then any of the other Gospels and Jesus trusted John so much that He gave John the care of his mother. John 19:26-27 "When Jesus therefore saw His mother, and the disciple whom He loved standing by, He said to His mother, "Woman, behold your son!" Then He said to the disciple, "Behold your mother!" And from that hour that disciple took her to his own home." As the oldest son, He was responsible for His mother's care. Hanging on the cross, about to die, He knew He would not be able to fulfill that responsibility. So, His most important human responsibility on earth, He entrusted to John.

   d. So, Jesus showed us that we can trust certain people if they prove themselves to be trustworthy. What we need to be willing to do, is to give them the opportunities to prove their trustworthiness. If they prove themselves to be trustworthy then we can trust them, if they do not, then we need to wise enough to not put our trust in them.

Loving by Faith Journal
Week 13

Choose **ONE** of the steps of Love always allowing itself to be persuaded to put our confidence in and rely on the object of that love and discuss how you feel about that step, what God may have shown you regarding that step and how you will incorporate that step into your life.

1. Make a conscious decision to allow God to persuade you that He is trustworthy and then act on that decision.

2. Make a conscious decision to believe that God will give you opportunities to persuade Him that you are trustworthy and act on that decision.

3. Make a conscious decision to persuade yourself that you are trustworthy (only if your thoughts and actions line up with Scripture) and then act on that decision.

4. Make a conscious decision to allow other people to persuade you that they are trustworthy and then act on that decision.

Week 14

– Love always hopes

I. If we are to love by faith, then we need to understand what love is.

   A. To understand what love is we must look at 1 Corinthians 13:4-8a "Love is patient, love is kind. It does not envy, it does not boast, it is not proud. It does not dishonor others, it is not self-seeking, it is not easily angered, and it keeps no record of wrongs. Love does not delight in evil but rejoices with the truth. It always protects, always trusts, always hopes, and always perseveres. Love never fails."

   B. Each week we will examine each aspect of love in these verses and apply the four-step process to each aspect.

II. This week we will look at the fact that Love always hopes.

   A. The Greek word for hope is *elpís* (from *elpō*, "to anticipate, welcome") – properly, expectation of what is sure (certain); hope.

   B. I love the word 'anticipate'. That word gives me a picture of a child sitting on the edge of their chair, eagerly waiting for something that they know will bring them great joy. I see the same picture when I think of love always hoping or anticipating the best.

   C. But this type of hoping is more than just anticipating something. It is also welcoming that something when it comes to us. With the word, 'welcome' I see a child who has been eagerly awaiting a Christmas present and then her mom tells her to close her eyes and hold out her arms. Her mother places a new puppy in her arms and the child squeals and welcomes the new puppy with hugs and kisses. This is the picture I see in my mind when I think of the words 'anticipate' and 'welcome'. Love should be just like that child, always anticipating something wonderful and then welcoming that something wonderful with open arms.

   D. So, the definition of hope is to always be anticipating something good and then welcome that good with open arms when it happens.

   E. Let's apply this definition of hope to the four-step process.

1. Make a conscious decision to believe that God is anticipating you and will welcome you with open arms when you give yourself to Him and act on that decision.
   a. The best picture of how God is hoping and anticipating us is the "Prodigal Son" parable in Luke 15:11-32.
   b. Luke 15:20 "And he arose and came to his father. But when he was still a great way off, his father saw him and had compassion, and ran and fell on his neck and kissed him." This son's father saw him coming and ran out to greet him. He was highly anticipating his son's return and welcomed his son home with open arms.
   c. This is how God is waiting and watching and hoping for us to return to Him.
2. Make a conscious decision to anticipate God working in your life through His Word and welcome His work and His Words with open arms and act on that decision.
   a. Psalm 48:14 "For this is God, Our God forever and ever; He will be our guide even to death." If we anticipate that God will guide us, then He will. But we need to be willing to follow His guidance
   b. 1 John 1:9 "If we confess our sins, He is faithful and just to forgive us our sins and to cleanse us from all unrighteousness." We can anticipate that God will forgive our sins and cleanse us from all the unrighteousness of those sins, but we must first be willing to confess our sins to Him.
   c. James 1:5 "If any of you lacks wisdom, let him ask of God, who gives to all liberally and without reproach, and it will be given to him." If we don't know what to do in a situation we can anticipate that God will show us what we should do but we must ask and keep asking and then learn to listen.
3. Make a conscious decision to anticipate God's best in your life and welcome God's best with open arms and act on that decision.

a. Ephesians 1:3 "Blessed be the God and Father of our Lord Jesus Christ, who has blessed us with every spiritual blessing in the heavenly places in Christ" God will give us every Spiritual blessing. Notice that word Spiritual. This means it may not always be material blessings. God will give us material blessings, but He is more concerned about the state of our souls than He is with our material wealth.

b. John 10:10 "The thief does not come except to steal, and to kill, and to destroy. I have come that they may have life, and that they may have it more abundantly." Jesus came to give us abundant life. That means all of life; emotional, mental, spiritual, and physical. He wants us to be well rounded whole people.

c. Proverbs 10:22 "The blessing of the Lord makes one rich, And He adds no sorrow with it." God does want to provide for our needs, but He does not want us to have the sorrow that comes with material blessings gotten the wrong way.

d. Matthew 6:33 "But seek first the kingdom of God and His righteousness, and all these things shall be added to you." Many people put the emphasis on the last part of this verse, but I believe God intended for us to put the emphasis on the first part. When we put His kingdom first then God can add all these things to us without any sorrow.

4. Make a conscious decision to anticipate God's best for other people and help them to welcome God's best with open arms and act on that decision.

a. 1 Corinthians 12:26 "And if one member suffers, all the members suffer with it; or if one member is honored, all the members rejoice with it." When something good happens to another person, we should rejoice with them.

b. Galatians 6:2 "Bear one another's burdens, and so fulfill the law of Christ." Life can be difficult, so we need to be willing to bear one another's burdens as well as rejoice with those who rejoice.

c. Hebrews 10:24-25 "And let us consider one another in order to stir up love and good works, not forsaking the assembling of ourselves together, as is the manner of some, but exhorting one another, and so much the more as you see the Day approaching." Many people quote "not forsaking the assembling of ourselves together" as a way to guilt people into being in a Church service on Sunday mornings but when we delve deeper into these verses we see that the Church is supposed to be a place of relationship, in which we "consider one another in order to stir up love and good works". If Church is only about sitting in a pew watching a show on stage, then we miss the whole point of what the Bible says Church should be.

d. Ephesians 3:14-19 "For this reason I bow my knees to the Father of our Lord Jesus Christ, from whom the whole family in heaven and earth is named, that He would grant you, according to the riches of His glory, to be strengthened with might through His Spirit in the inner man, that Christ may dwell in your hearts through faith; that you, being rooted and grounded in love, may be able to comprehend with all the saints what is the width and length and depth and height—to know the love of Christ which passes knowledge; that you may be filled with all the fullness of God." This is true anticipation of God's best for people.

e. When we suffer with people and bear their burdens with them and then rejoice with them when things are going well and always stir them up to love and good works then we are anticipating God's best for their lives and helping them to accept God's best for their lives.

Amy Leigh Moore

Loving by Faith Journal

Week 14

Choose **ONE** of the steps of Love is always anticipating something good and then welcoming that good with open arms when it happens and discuss how you feel about that step, what God may have shown you regarding that step and how you will incorporate that step into your life.

1. Make a conscious decision to believe that God is anticipating you and will welcome you with open arms when you give yourself to Him and act on that decision.

2. Make a conscious decision to anticipate God working in your life through His Word and welcome His work and His Words with open arms and act on that decision.

3. Make a conscious decision to anticipate God's best in your life and welcome God's best with open arms and act on that decision.

4. Make a conscious decision to anticipate God's best for other people and help them to welcome God's best with open arms and act on that decision.

Week 15

– Love always perseveres

I. If we are to love by faith, then we need to understand what love is.

   A. To understand what love is we must look at 1 Corinthians 13:4-8a "Love is patient, love is kind. It does not envy, it does not boast, it is not proud. It does not dishonor others, it is not self-seeking, it is not easily angered, and it keeps no record of wrongs. Love does not delight in evil but rejoices with the truth. It always protects, always trusts, always hopes, and always perseveres. Love never fails."

   B. Each week we will examine each aspect of love in these verses and apply the four-step process to each aspect.

II. This week we will look at the fact that Love always perseveres.

   A. The Greek word for perseverance is *hypomonḗ* (from 5259 /*hypó*, "under" and 3306 /*ménō*, "remain, endure") – properly, remaining under, endurance; steadfastness, especially as God enables the believer to "remain (endure) under" the challenges He allots in life.

   B. This is the same word that is used for patience. So being patient and persevering are closely related. But there is a difference. So, what is the difference?

   C. The English definition for patience is "the ability to accept delay, suffering, or annoyance without complaining or becoming angry". This definition is passive. It does not require much action on the part of the patient person. That does not mean it is not important. Without patience we can't persevere. So, what is perseverance?

   D. The definition of perseverance is "continued effort and determination". So, perseverance is actionable, whereas patience is not. Perseverance continues on despite obstacles and setbacks. It never gives up, no matter what.

   E. So, Love will always continue despite obstacles and setbacks. Love never gives up. Because Love will never give up then it will never fail.

   F. Let's apply that definition of perseverance to the four-step process.

1. Make a conscious decision to believe that God's love for you will continue despite obstacles and setbacks and that God will never give up on you and that His Love never fails and then act on that decision.

    a. Hebrews 13:5 "Let your conduct be without covetousness; be content with such things as you have. For He Himself has said, "I will never leave you nor forsake you." No matter what we go through, God will always be there.

    b. Philippians 1:6 "Being confident of this very thing, that He who has begun a good work in you will complete it until the day of Jesus Christ" God has started a work in you and He will not give up until that work is complete.

    c. Hebrews 12:2 "Looking unto Jesus, the author and finisher of our faith, who for the joy that was set before Him endured the cross, despising the shame, and has sat down at the right hand of the throne of God." Jesus is not only the author of our faith but He will also finish our faith. He will stay with us through everything life can throw at us so that our faith will be complete.

2. Make a conscious decision that your love for God will continue despite obstacles and setbacks and that you will never give up your love for God and then act on that decision.

    a. Psalm 16:8 "I have set the Lord always before me; Because He is at my right hand I shall not be moved." David did not have an easy life. He was hunted by King Saul because Saul was threatened by him and wanted to kill him. Having a king want to kill you would be enough for anyone to sink into despair yet David refused to let despair and depression take a hold in his heart. He kept his love for God at the forefront of his thoughts and refused to walk away from that love no matter what happened in his life.

    b. Job 13:15 "Though He slay me, yet will I trust Him. Even so, I will defend my own ways before Him." Job had lost everything in his life, yet he says that He will still trust God despite losing everything. Job's friends had told him that God had taken everything from him as a punishment for some sin he had committed, and this was part of Job's answer to them. He told them that even if God was to slay him, he would still trust God. His love for God would persevere no matter what happened.

3. Make a conscious decision that your dreams will continue despite obstacles and setbacks and that you will never give up on the plan God has for your life and act on that decision.

   a. Jeremiah 29:11 New International Version (NIV) "For I know the plans I have for you," declares the Lord, "plans to prosper you and not to harm you, plans to give you hope and a future." God has a plan for your life and it is up to you to learn what that plan is and then never give up on that plan.

   b. Galatians 6:9 "And let us not grow weary while doing good, for in due season we shall reap if we do not lose heart." Other translations say, "if we do not give up". We must keep on going no matter what and believe that God will work everything out for us in the way that is best for us. But to see that happen we can't give up on God's plan for our lives.

   c. Joshua 1:9 "Have I not commanded you? Be strong and of good courage; do not be afraid, nor be dismayed, for the Lord your God is with you wherever you go." Since God is with us wherever we go then we can be strong and courageous and no give up when times get tough.

4. Make a conscious decision that you will continue for the people you love despite obstacles and setbacks and you will never give up on the people you love and act on that decision.

   a. Romans 12:10 New International Version (NIV) "Be devoted to one another in love. Honor one another above yourselves."

   b. The Greek word for devotion is *proskartereō* (from *prós*, "towards, interactively with" and *kartereō*, "show steadfast strength," derived from 2904 /*krátos*, "prevailing strength") – properly, to consistently showing strength which prevails (in spite of difficulties); to endure (remain firm), staying in a fixed direction. "To continue to do something with intense effort, with the possible implication of despite difficulty – 'to devote oneself to, to keep on, to persist in'"

    c.   So, if we are to be devoted to one another we should endure with one another despite the difficulties that will come with that devotion. When we learn to love like that then our love will never fail.

III. Learning how to love must be one of the building blocks of the Church. If we do not know how to love, then however we build the Church, it is doomed to failure and many more people will experience Church hurt. Without the knowledge of how to love then our Churches become places of empty ritual and not places of healthy relationships. Empty ritual then becomes a religion and Jesus hated religion. Religion is about rules and regulations and what Jesus died to give us was much more then ritual. He died an excruciating death so that we could have true relationship with Him and one another based on these 13 different aspects of Love. We cannot truly live the way God wants us to live without knowing how to love.

Matthew 22:37-40 "Jesus said to him, '"You shall love the Lord your God with all your heart, with all your soul, and with all your mind.' This is the first and great commandment. And the second is like it: 'You shall love your neighbor as yourself.' On these two commandments hang all the Law and the Prophets."

Amy Leigh Moore

Loving by Faith Journal
Week 15

Choose **ONE** of the steps of Love is always anticipating something good and then welcoming that good with open arms when it happens and discuss how you feel about that step, what God may have shown you regarding that step and how you will incorporate that step into your life.

1. Make a conscious decision to believe that God's love for you will continue despite obstacles and setbacks and that God will never give up on you and that His Love never fails and then act on that decision.

2. Make a conscious decision that your love for God will continue despite obstacles and setbacks and that you will never give up your love for God and then act on that decision.

3. Make a conscious decision that your dreams will continue despite obstacles and setbacks and that you will never give up on the plan God has for your life and act on that decision.

4. Make a conscious decision that your love for people will continue despite obstacles and setbacks and you will never give up on the people you love and act on that decision.

Amy Leigh Moore

End Notes

Hull, B. (2014). *The complete book of discipleship: On being and making followers of Christ.* Carol Stream, IL: Tyndale House Publishers, Inc.

Lead | Definition & Pronunciation of Lead by Merriam-Webster. (n.d.). Retrieved from https://www.merriam-webster.com/dictionary/lead

Millions of Unchurched Adults Are Christians Hurt by Churches but Can Be Healed of the Pain. (2010, April 12). Retrieved from https://www.barna.org/barna-update/faith-spirituality/362-millions-of-unchurched-adults-are-christians-hurt-by-churches-but-can-be-healed-of-the-pain#.VlTVwDZdE2w

Cornerstone | Definition of Cornerstone by Merriam-Webster. (n.d.). Retrieved from https://www.merriam-webster.com/dictionary/cornerstone

Strong's Greek: 204. ἀκρογωνιαῖος (akrogóniaios) -- at the extreme angle or corner. (n.d.). Retrieved from http://biblehub.com/greek/204.htm

Strong's Hebrew: 6438. פִּנָּה (pinnah) -- a corner. (n.d.). Retrieved from http://biblehub.com/hebrew/6438.htm

Strong's Greek: 2099. εὐαγγελιστής (euaggelistés) -- an evangelist, a bringer of good news. (n.d.). Retrieved from http://biblehub.com/greek/2099.htm

Strong's Greek: 652. ἀπόστολος (apostolos) -- a messenger, one sent on a mission, an apostle. (n.d.). Retrieved from http://biblehub.com/greek/652.htm

Strong's Greek: 4396. προφήτης (prophétés) -- a prophet (an interpreter or forth-teller of the divine will). (n.d.). Retrieved from http://www.biblehub.com/greek/4396.htm

Strong's Greek: 1321. διδάσκω (didaskó) -- to teach. (n.d.). Retrieved from http://biblehub.com/greek/1321.htm

Strong's Greek: 3100. μαθητεύω (mathéteuó) -- to be a disciple, to make a disciple. (n.d.). Retrieved from http://biblehub.com/greek/3100.htm

Strong's Greek: 4166. ποιμήν (poimén) -- a shepherd. (n.d.). Retrieved from http://biblehub.com/greek/4166.htm

Shepherd - Easton's Bible Dictionary Online. (n.d.). Retrieved from http://www.biblestudytools.com/dictionaries/eastons-bible-dictionary/shepherd.html

Clergy as Mandatory Reporters of Child abuse and neglect. (2015, August). Retrieved from https://www.childwelfare.gov/pubPDFs/clergymandated.pdf

McLeod, S. (2016). Maslow's Hierarchy of Needs | Simply Psychology. Retrieved from http://www.simplypsychology.org/maslow.html

Shook, J. S. (2012). *Making housing happen: Faith-based affordable housing models* (2nd ed.). Eugene, OR: Cascade Books.

Strong's Greek: 941. βαστάζω (bastazó) -- to take up, carry. (n.d.). Retrieved from http://biblehub.com/greek/941.htm

Pastor Burnout Statistics. (n.d.). Retrieved from http://www.pastorburnout.com/pastor-burnout-statistics.html

Strong's Hebrew: 2964. טָרָף (tereph) -- prey, food, a leaf. (n.d.). Retrieved from http://biblehub.com/hebrew/2964.htm

Giving Statistics: Charity Navigator. (2017). Retrieved from http://www.charitynavigator.org/index.cfm/bay/content.view/cpid/42#.VjmV3DZdHg9

A Love without Condition - History of the Early Church - Early Church.com. (n.d.). Retrieved from http://www.earlychurch.com/unconditional-love.php

Understanding Anemia. (2008, December 14). Retrieved from http://www.webmd.com/a-to-zguides/understanding-anemia-symptoms

Kee, H. C. (2005). Medicine, miracle and magic in New Testament times. Cambridge: Cambridge University Press.

Strong's Greek: 5281. ὑπομονή (hupomoné) -- a remaining behind, a patient enduring. (n.d.). Retrieved from http://biblehub.com/greek/5281.htm

End Notes

Patient | Definition of Patient by Merriam-Webster. (n.d.). Retrieved from https://www.merriam-webster.com/dictionary/patient

Strong's Hebrew: 6960. קָוָה (qavah) -- wait. (n.d.). Retrieved from http://biblehub.com/hebrew/6960.htm

Wickstrom, S. P. (n.d.). Wait upon the Lord. Retrieved from http://www.spwickstrom.com/wait/

Strong's Greek: 941. βαστάζω (bastazó) -- to take up, carry. (n.d.). Retrieved from http://biblehub.com/greek/941.htm

Strong's Greek: 5544. χρηστότης (chréstotés) -- goodness, excellence, uprightness. (n.d.). Retrieved from http://biblehub.com/greek/5544.htm

Strong's Greek: 5485. χάρις (charis) -- grace, kindness. (n.d.). Retrieved from http://biblehub.com/greek/5485.htm

Strong's Greek: 5355. φθόνος (phthonos) -- envy. (n.d.). Retrieved from http://biblehub.com/greek/5355.htm

Strong's Greek: 2206. ζηλόω (zéloó) -- to be jealous. (n.d.). Retrieved from http://biblehub.com/greek/2206.htm

Definition of JEALOUSY. (n.d.). Retrieved from http://www.merriam-webster.com/dictionary/jealousy

Strong's Greek: 4352. προσκυνέω (proskuneó) -- to do reverence to. (n.d.). Retrieved from http://biblehub.com/greek/4352.htm

Strong's Greek: 2745. καύχημα (kauchéma) -- a boast. (n.d.). Retrieved from http://biblehub.com/greek/2745.htm

Strong's Greek: 2744. καυχάομαι (kauchaomai) -- to boast. (n.d.). Retrieved from http://biblehub.com/greek/2744.htm

Definition of BOAST. (n.d.). Retrieved from http://www.merriam-webster.com/dictionary/boast

Strong's Greek: 5243. *ὑπερηφανία* (huperéphania) -- haughtiness, disdain. (n.d.). Retrieved from http://biblehub.com/greek/5243.htm

Strong's Greek: 5244. *ὑπερήφανος* (huperephanos) -- proud, arrogant. (n.d.). Retrieved from http://biblehub.com/greek/5244.htm

Strong's Greek: 5012. *ταπεινοφροσύνη* (tapeinophrosune) -- humility. (n.d.). Retrieved from http://biblehub.com/greek/5012.htm

Strong's Greek: 5092. *τιμή* (timé) -- a valuing, a price. (n.d.). Retrieved from http://biblehub.com/greek/5092.htm

Strong's Greek: 1391. *δόξα* (doxa) -- opinion (always good in N.T.), hence praise, honor, glory. (n.d.). Retrieved from http://biblehub.com/greek/1391.htm

Strong's Greek: 2052. *ἐριθεία* (eritheia) -- rivalry, hence ambition. (n.d.). Retrieved from http://biblehub.com/greek/2052.htm

Definition of SELFISH. (n.d.). Retrieved from https://www.merriam-webster.com/dictionary/selfish

Strong's Greek: 2212. *ζητέω* (zéteó) -- to seek. (n.d.). Retrieved from http://biblehub.com/greek/2212.htm

Bailey, D. S. (2006, June). Burnout harms workers' physical health through many pathways. Retrieved from http://www.apa.org/monitor/jun06/burnout.aspx

Strong's Greek: 3709. *ὀργή* (orgé) -- impulse, wrath. (n.d.). Retrieved from http://biblehub.com/greek/3709.htm

Strong's Greek: 5083. *τηρέω* (téreó) -- to watch over, to guard. (n.d.). Retrieved from http://biblehub.com/greek/5083.htm

Strong's Greek: 5483. *χαρίζομαι* (charizomai) -- to show favor, give freely. (n.d.). Retrieved from http://biblehub.com/greek/5483.htm

Strong's Greek: 4190. *πονηρός* (ponéros) -- toilsome, bad. (n.d.). Retrieved from http://biblehub.com/greek/4190.htm

End Notes

Strong's Greek: 225. ἀλήθεια (alétheia) -- truth. (n.d.). Retrieved from http://biblehub.com/greek/225.htm

Strong's Greek: 5442. φυλάσσω (phulassó) -- to guard, watch. (n.d.). Retrieved from http://biblehub.com/greek/5442.htm

Strong's Greek: 5083. τηρέω (téreó) -- to watch over, to guard. (n.d.). Retrieved from http://biblehub.com/greek/5083.htm

Strong's Greek: 4102. πίστις (pistis) -- faith, faithfulness. (n.d.). Retrieved from http://biblehub.com/greek/4102.htm

John: Jesus' Trusted Disciple - Joy Magazine. (2007, September). Retrieved from http://www.joymag.co.za/article.php?id=121

Strong's Greek: 1680. ἐλπίς (elpis) -- expectation, hope. (n.d.). Retrieved from http://biblehub.com/greek/1680.htm

Patience Definition in the Cambridge English Dictionary. (n.d.). Retrieved from http://dictionary.cambridge.org/us/dictionary/english/patience

Perseverance Definition in the Cambridge English Dictionary. (n.d.). Retrieved from http://dictionary.cambridge.org/us/dictionary/english/perseverance

Strong's Greek: 4342. προσκαρτερέω (proskartereó) -- to attend constantly. (n.d.). Retrieved from http://biblehub.com/greek/4342.htm

For more information contact:

Amy Leigh Moore
C/O Advantage Books
P.O. Box 160847
Altamonte Springs, FL 32716

info@advbooks.com

To purchase additional copies of this book visit our bookstore website at: www.advbookstore.com

Longwood, Florida, USA
"we bring dreams to life"™
www.advbookstore.com

www.ingramcontent.com/pod-product-compliance
Lightning Source LLC
Chambersburg PA
CBHW062204080426
42734CB00010B/1784